Gary Troia

I Return to Versions of Myself

Gary Troia

OTHER BOOKS BY GARY TROIA

Spanish Yarns and Beyond

A Bricklayer's Tales

English Yarns and Beyond

The Complete Short Stories of Gary Troia

Coach to Como

Ray Dennis Does *The Secret*

Through The Porthole

ULOpia

Baby on Board

New York and Back

I Return to Versions of Myself

Gary Troia

CONTENTS

I Return to Versions of Myself

Gary Troia

I Return to Versions of Myself

Gary Troia

A Reckoning

What a wee little part of a person's life are his acts and his words! His real life is led in his head, and is known to none but himself.

Autobiography of Mark Twain, Volume 1

What can the England of 1940 have in common with the England of 1840? But then, what have you in common with the child of five whose photograph your mother keeps on the mantlepiece? Nothing, except that you happen to be the same person.

George Orwell

Introduction

Not everything I'm going to write can be true. Trying to recapture feelings and meanings of vanished versions will be tentative at best, or way off target at worst. For much of my life I've hidden some versions of myself in dark areas within my mind, like wretched prisoners of war, abandoned and rejected by their own kind. I supposed they must not be shown to the world, or I would find myself under unnecessary scrutiny. Yet sometimes I ventured there to shine a light on a forgotten face or two. When I looked into their eyes, each one implored me to release them, but I resisted. I have been fearful of this day, but now it's time to free them all as they have done enough time, and after all, without them I would not be able to tell the tale, and without them, I would not be me.

Some versions I recall are seen clearly in my mind from a remote vantage point. Others are unseen, but I feel them. Then there are those I remember by the consequences of their actions, while others are so familiar that I can still see through their eyes without a tick or a tock of any time lost, as if *I* were living through them once again.

Deep in my heart resides the authentic *me*: genuine and true. I fit in anywhere and everywhere because I am in alignment with myself. Yet from the spokes that radiate from my centre are found all manner of entities, characteristics, moods, personalities, and demons – an array of versions of myself. Apart from these there stands alone an imposter that has thwarted me from the outset, and I've never been able to lock *it* up. It hardly ever reveals *itself*, but when *it* does, there is nothing I can do to deter *it*. It comes with a feeling of ruinous emptiness, licking *its* lips at limitless possibilities that overstep accepted social boundaries. When *it* steps forward into *my* space *it* brings a crackle of dark energy, generated by the power of complete disregard for the consequences of *its* actions. *It* tries to bring me down, but *it* fails because I resist.

As I end this introduction, and before I cast off, it is safe to say that there are many things wrong with me, but fewer than before. My behaviour was often inappropriate, but it's better than before. My mind has caused me pain, but less so than before.

So, this was *our* journey, more or less...

Part 1

Gary Troia

Chapter 1

Don't judge each day by the harvest you reap, but by the seeds
you plant.
Robert Louis Stevenson

I was born in southeast London to a working-class family. My father drove for a living and my mother worked in central London as a PA to an executive.

Those early years were the most bewildering of all, living with a family that became each day more familiar and stranger in equal measure. Not just that, but I didn't know who I was, and nor did I know my destination. Then, *they* set a path. And if you are not careful, you become *their* future in a continuous loop of mind-numbing familial mediocrity and hopelessness, nothing more than a facsimile of *them*; but I remember with clarity and precision a place away from that: my nursery school.

It's a lovely place. There is an old black car in the

playground. We take turns driving it to magical places. At night I dream of where we can go tomorrow. Every morning I enter the nursery and hang my bag and coat on a hook (a red squirrel above it depicts mine). We spend the morning playing and running and jumping and painting and laughing. In the afternoon we all have a drink and a biscuit, then the teachers set out little camp beds with red tartan blankets and close the curtains. We rest on our beds in the dark. One of the teachers reads a story. I like this time because my parents never read to me. I feel sorry for them because they don't know about magical things. The stories show me worlds better than mine. Strange and interesting things happen in them, disappointing and mundane things happen in mine.

I feel cold in the warm sunshine walking home after they tell me that nursery school has ended for ever.

I Return to Versions of Myself

Gary Troia

Chapter 2

You do not want to be another self.

A Course in Miracles

My primary and junior schools were combined in an old brick building in sight of the nursery. Often, I would wistfully look out a classroom window at my happy place just down the road and hanker after those fast-receding good times.

A few events stand out after the nursery version turned into the primary school one. The first was getting into the small plastic swimming pool for the first time - I was more excited than nervous. I'd never been swimming before. Whenever we were in the playground, I kept looking at the building with the pool in it. The Annex they called it. I used to yearn for the day when our class moved up a year to be able to use it.

The day that once seemed so far away, arrived. We

got changed. I remember the tension within me building and the smell of chlorine in my nostrils. We stood in lines of three. The first three got in and splashed their way to the end and back. Soon I was standing on the right-hand side of three at the edge of the water. The instructor told us what to do. I'd seen some others wade or kneel their way along. I was bursting with anticipation. We jumped in and the teacher shouted: "Go"! I dived forward, palms padding along the bottom. Instinct took over. My hands left the light blue plastic, making ungainly strokes forward - I was sort of swimming. I looked to my left and saw I was way ahead of the other two.

Joy welled up in me. I reached the end and looked at the instructor. The other two were still splashing and crawling along. The instructor said, "Well, what are you waiting for"? I pushed off the end of the pool with my feet and swam even better on the return length. The instructor gave me praise. I was elated. It was the first time in my life I had done something well enough to warrant praise.

At Christmas, just before the holidays, our class made

outfits out of cardboard and then glued red and green tinfoil onto them. One group in green was going to march beside the other group in red. The teacher asked which colour the leader should wear. I went inwards because I desperately wanted to come up with an answer. I surprised myself when I blurted out: "The one in the front should be half red and half green". The look in the teacher's eyes told me that she was genuinely impressed by my answer. Later, I wore the breastplate of red and green tin foil with pride.

Another defining event was with my father, who must have been lumbered with me for the day. It wasn't until somewhere down the line I found out that he *really* liked the ladies. He liked them very much. In fact, he liked them so much that he took me to meet one: Something's not right. Everything's not right. I don't know this house. I don't like this house because it feels like it does when I open the big freezer to get a lolly. The woman is trying to be friendly, but I just want to go home. Why are they giggling? What's so funny? I wish I was in my bedroom with my toys and teddy bear. The clock on the mantelpiece ticks too loudly. She has finished being friendly to me. They go upstairs. I stay in the living room. They've left sweets and comics.

In the car on the way home, I do not like my dad. He doesn't like me.

From that day on, whenever he had an opportunity, he clipped his hand on the back of my head. Mostly what I thought about when I was around him was this: One day I will be big enough and strong enough to take you on and beat you.

Later, I sensed the light *outside* dim a little, as if *someone* stepped in front of me and closed a shutter on an untrustworthy world *out there*.

I Return to Versions of Myself

Gary Troia

Chapter 3

A person's a person no matter how small.

Dr. Seuss

At junior school I became aware of something emerging within me. It was elusive then and remains so now, but it seemed to be the authentic me, or at least an essence of me that was all my own. Even back then it was like remembering who I truly am. I let it flourish and have fun. Life became effortless. I became playful and popular, easy-going and free. Goodwill and opportunities orbited me like I was the Sun of my own solar system.

I had a friend. We devised a secret code. He dropped notes through my letterbox before school and I would try to decode them before I got to school. For most of the early years we lived in a council flat close to the school, but soon my parents bought a semi-detached house and a greengrocer shop, and so, for once my father deviated from driving, because up until then he mainly drove ambulances and buses. The shop stood at the bottom of the hill from my school.

One day I saw a new delivery. In a small box were dark reddish fruits, which I'd never seen before. They turned out to be pomegranates. I took a couple to school - not to eat myself, but to present them to girls I liked. On the way up the hill, I felt like an explorer, returning home from a voyage to unchartered lands. I felt I was offering the girls a whole new experience into the world of exotic fruit. Often, I would arrive at school and start speaking a foreign language because I was multi-lingual – at least in my mind. I sensed then and now that none of this was to impress or show off, it was just an honest attempt at being joyful and entertaining.

I used to be allowed to a friend's house on a Wednesday after school. Across from his house was a field. A group of us used to play football there. Our ball got kicked away from our immediate game area.

I still see that scene from a remote viewing point.

There is nothing I can do to help, as that little version retrieves the ball, he is grabbed by the arms of an odious beast. I viscerally sense that *thing* licking my face, smelling once again the vile odour of his hellish breath. He jerks suddenly with me in his arms, moving towards the woods. Instincts take over and that little heroic version kicks the nonce hard in the groin. *He* winces but holds on. The little version screams for help. His friends rush over and start to kick the ogre in the legs until he lets go. We chase *him* a short distance, kicking *him* in the back of the legs, throwing stones at *him* before *he* merges with the wood from where *he* likely came.

That little version is standing shocked, not able to comprehend adult behaviour anymore. The beast looked monstrous as he lurched away supernaturally fast without breaking into a run. I suppose he was practiced at trying not to draw attention to himself as he made his frequent getaways. That version went home and told no one; it was the last time for a long time any version would have uninterrupted joy of life. Once again *someone* seemed to move forward and slam down a couple more shutters, dimming the world again. For years after I detested kissing just in case a woman's breath had turned enough to be reminiscent of that monster's putrid saliva.

By now I was swimming early in the morning before school and again after it had finished. It brought me discipline. I felt fit, strong and healthy. I competed for district teams and then at national level. It came easy to me. I liked swimming because it was fun, free and meditative. It was coming home after training when I noticed a huge dip in energy. There were constant arguments when my father was there, but they never lasted long as he was always keen and eager for a way out to meet new ladies.

When my swimming moved to another level, he somehow managed to manoeuvre himself into driving the team bus to venues. I saw how proud and important he felt - not for me - for himself. He had never been remotely interested before, yet here he was giving his free time to driving the team to events. I watched him talking to coaches and other parents, deep in conversation about swimming, like he had led the way as some innovative trainer. I decided to stop swimming to puncture and deflate his unearned pride. This was when he changed further towards me. He despised me for tarnishing his unearned glory, and it took me a long time to realise that he couldn't cope with his child turning against him, so he turned against his child.

Soon after he left the house never to return.

Gary Troia

Chapter 4

"– choice, not chance, determines your destiny."

Aristotle

My secondary school was an accursed place. If you wanted a life in crime, then it was a wonderful finishing school, but for anything else it was close to useless. You could fight every day without punishment. Steal money off the weaker ones and intimidate the teachers without any punishment. I thought that education would get more interesting as I rose through the system, whereas this school was more of a survival course unless you were committed to disruption.

I somehow managed to walk a line that carried me through with the least number of problems. I knew all the troublemakers and had a rapport with them, connected with the decent kids, and was close to some of the good-looking, intelligent girls; but none of the relationships went anywhere below surface level; maybe the best analogy to depict my schooling was like watching a balloon floating by a window: it just passed.

I did judo once a week in the hope of learning self-defence and discipline. One evening I couldn't get a lift home so one of the judo instructors offered to drive me, he put his hand on my groin as we waited at traffic lights. I was enraged. I screamed "CUNT", jumped out of the car and gave him a look that was so full of venom that he turned away and drove off as fast as he could. That focused level of violence I experienced staring at him gave me a brief insight of what a Spartan warrior might have felt at the battle of Thermopylae: no thought of backing down even though you know you're going to lose by sheer weight of numbers against you, or in my case, a child against a well-built adult with a black belt in judo. I went home that evening, something changed within. I decided that people in authority were not to be trusted. Adults were weak and hypocritical and had no idea about life at all. Real life I mean, the deeper truths, not the day-to-day surface froth of kidding everyone on with a loose, ill-fitting mask.

I see now that this was probably the pivotal point where I separated myself from everything *out there*. In a way I had created something new within me, or let *something* in, because I heard a distinctive voice state loud and clear: "Nothing like this will ever happen to *us* again. It will not be permitted". I can tell you now that voice gave me some comfort.

The defence I'd set up to keep guard from the dangers of adults *out there* actually moved in and moved *me* out of the way. And I was glad to take a back seat. But it was like inviting the mafia in to help. I now had feared protection, although it was likely I would pay a hefty price for it somewhere along the way, but right then I just needed some protection because I didn't feel safe. Many versions from that decision on would hardly ever experience peace and joy, some would never experience it at all, just successive moments of life happening either with strife or without it. Being without strife briefly seemed to be the best I could hope for.

From then on, I could never be sure who had my best interests. Almost always the attack dog within me scared off any good Samaritan, as it reminded me of the past, and the past was not going to repeat itself. And it didn't, nothing like that ever happened again, but the price was high, and many demons began to pile on in.

By now I was only interested in extreme behaviour that brought nothing but pain to me, causing a knock-on effect to anyone close. Gone was the carefree multilingual explorer bearing exotic fruits. My mum was calling me a rebel without a cause. I looked suspiciously upon anyone with authority – and very few had it in that secondary school. Most of the teachers were not there for long, as they must have found it such an unworkable environment. I never read one book there. I had no guidance at home because my mother was working two jobs now that father had scarpered. I rattled loudly in an empty silent house save for a white noise that hummed away and never ceased. I delighted at being in the wrong crowd. The authentic child I used to be had left home, replaced by a suspicious lookout.

Invariably a friend and I would do something wrong in class, so we were thrown out and had to sit with our Heads of Houses. My friend's Head of House was an aggressive stout woman who seemed to have escaped from a Charles Dickens' novel. Mine was a young, stylish woman. For punishment I sat in her office and put her class books in alphabetical order. I preferred this to being in a rowdy class that the teacher couldn't control. She wore miniskirts. I used to pretend to read but kept glancing at her legs. Sometimes she drove me home. I pretended we were married. I found out where she lived. I used to cycle to her house. It was about ten minutes' ride. I used to circle around outside. Sometimes she saw me through her front window. It's embarrassing thinking of it now, but I'm almost sure she understood that I was just looking for someone to guide me; at least that is what I still tell myself to relieve the itchy embarrassment.

I started doing drugs and drinking after school in the park. I never did one piece of homework, yet no one contacted my mother. I stopped going for the most part and still no one said anything. We retired to a park shed in the evening, getting pissed on *Olde English Cider* and smoking. It started out with cheap cider and gravitated towards anything that gave a high or buzz. We even poured plaster remover onto hankies and sniffed them. I stopped sniffing after looking at the ceiling in a friend's bedroom when I saw two nicotine-coloured patches above each of our heads that weren't there before we started.

In the daytime I often met up with the other wasters in the abandoned Arsenal, a huge area where they made munitions in WW2. We drank and smoked, thought and talked about crime and anything destructive. There were many ideas put forward, but few stood the ultimate test of planning and action. One summer holiday, one idea did take hold. It was coming to the end of the summer holidays, and no one wanted to go back to school – although it was a ridiculous thought as none of us in the old air raid shelter went anyway. An idea to burn the school down was put forward. I listened without any belief that it might happen. But the idea gained momentum and five emerged who were going to carry out the attack. Elements needed for the arson attack were either bought or stolen. The night was chosen. A friend and I went to the top of a tower block opposite the school.

We waited…

Shadowy figures appeared before disappearing back into the dark. We detected an orange glow in the six-form block. It expanded until we could see proper flames with red in them. We took the lift down and headed for home as one siren became a cacophony of sirens.

All the fire starters were soon caught and sent to different institutions dependent on their age. The rest of us had an extended summer that really did feel like it would never end, while the school was refurbished.

This is how I stumbled through my time at school until one day was the last day. A day that filled me with dread, and as far as I could see, I was the only one, because I was the only one in no man's land. I was in a group of one. On the last day those who hated school were happy to be away and were never seen again. Some already had jobs. Others were just glad to be free. Yet here I was with those that were staying on to study. This group would no longer have to wear uniforms and they could study in peace, as all the disrupters (including me) were no more. I stayed all day with them as each one sorted out their studies.

On the way home I felt mentally destroyed and physically deflated. I was nudged into looking inside for an answer of what to do next, but unlike the primary school version that came to a considered answer by looking within, I found nothing there but emptiness. I yearned to be those young versions again, and I implored those little ones for help, for they were far more alive and much purer of soul than me, but they never came, and so the light dimmed once again like a bank of threatening clouds obscuring any hope that the sun might shine.

When I was old enough to see a doctor without my mother, I asked him if I could see someone whose expertise was *in* the mind rather than the body. It took some time to convince him, but a continual succession of irritating appointments urged him to agree.

I told the psychiatrist all I could with a limited vocabulary, but this is what I meant: "No matter what good comes my way, no matter if everything is right in my world, I am always anticipating that the worst is yet to come". The psychiatrist offered no insight.

The last two lines of William Ernest Henley's poem *Invictus*, "I am the master of my fate, I am the captain of my soul" has hardly ever been true for me. Many hands have held the helm through the years and charted unproductive courses. Some versions came to realise through reading and taking responsibility that they must retake the helm. A few have sailed their way through troubled seas and storms, while others were becalmed and even shipwrecked; still today there remains some unhelpful, mutinous crew on board. So, I try to remain vigilant and hold the course; but the open sea is a dangerous place.

I realise now that each version has tried to reclaim

that place that the primary version occupied, and wherever I was and whatever situation my mind was in was down to decisions made within. On that last walk home from school was the first time I recognised and named four of my mutinous crewmembers: disruption, distrust, vengeance, self-sabotage; and their captain was fear.

I Return to Versions of Myself

Gary Troia

Chapter 5

I also will conquer myself

Herman Hesse

Walking home after that last day of school was when all my defences slammed shut like a thick steel door of a prison cell, to keep all *out there* from getting in. I could hardly continue to walk, although I took a longer route to delay getting home. I had never felt so much self-doubt before. I had no direction. No discipline. No educational skills and no one in which I could confide. I never spoke to anyone about the paedophiles, my father's adulterous liaisons, nor did I mention the arson attack on the sixth form block. Somehow, I had acquired the code of *omertà* (unwritten law of silence).

Days went on in their shadowy familiar fashion. Occasionally I bumped into those of my year that had jobs and money, and others that had stayed on to learn. I knew I should do something, but I honestly did not know what to do or where to go. To make matters worse, I was seeing a girl who had stayed on, and every time we met, I felt the distance grow between us.

My mother introduced a new man into the home. At first, he came once a week. Then he never left. One night we were in his car and the moon was large and full. A conversation ensued about it, and it turned out that he thought the sun and the moon were the same thing but had different names depending on whether it was night or day. That was when I realised that there is no metamorphic switch from childhood wonder to adult wisdom, which up to then I was still banking on.

We moved away to a better area. A builder opposite was looking for a labourer. I worked on small extensions. I didn't like it but now I had money in my pocket. From there I got an apprenticeship in bricklaying. I didn't like that either, and all I could ever think about was how I had messed up my education and life. I didn't know what to do. I knew that I didn't want a life in construction, but I just didn't know how to get out of it. I started the apprenticeship and knew it was so wrong. The smell of cut brick, sand and mortar together is not a bad smell inherently, but it was one I did not like and came to loathe.

Laying those first few bricks, I turned on myself and started to dislike everything about where I was and who I was. I went through a significant list of figures and situations to blame, but as I went on, I grew weary to continue because I knew well enough that the last name on my list was mine, and although I pushed for more, for something else to attack, I could not see anyone or anything beyond myself.

One night a version came back from a party. He'd forgotten his key, so he knocked lightly on the door. He knocked again, and then slightly louder. The street was quiet, and he heard the new man say from the bedroom above, "Don't let him in, he should've taken his key. This will teach him a lesson".

For a few moments I waited outside and wondered

what to do. I just wanted to get to bed.

I knocked harder. I heard my mother, "Look, I'm just going to let him in".

The new man said "NO".

A battle was about to begin, and the best of all diplomats could not have prevented it.

Then, in the early morning quiet, I heard my brother speak out, "Look, this is a joke, I'm going down to let him in".

"Don't you dare", said the new man.

Outside I decided it was outrageous that a strange man would be telling my mother and brother not to open the door to me. My mother was not sticking up for me. And he was treating me like I didn't belong and believes that this is his house now. There was no more reflecting. I stood there and stepped aside for what seemed longer than it was. *He* was on his way, and *he* was looking forward to confrontation.

I heard my brother, "I'm going to open the door".

"Don't you dare", said the new man once again.

My brother came downstairs and let me in. The hope was that things would settle down and all would return to their slumber.

At the top of the stairs the new man stood. As I made it to the top of the landing, he began spouting cliches about respecting *his* house and the time. From that day on I have never been a great respecter of time. As he was ranting, I set a different course. All within became serene and calm. As he went on, the aggressive version was flexing and stretching. Calm thoughts in the inner space were thinking what could be done to create the biggest impact.

The new man was quite the home improver, having just built wardrobes in all the bedrooms. Then *he* arrived. *He* turned away from the ranting and went to the wardrobe and opened the door. Summoning up strength to make an immediate shock, *he* ripped it off its hinges. *He* was now standing with the door in *his* hands, smiling. That shut the new man up. The new man was opened-mouthed, aghast at what he had just witnessed. So, it was true what Caesar had said: *No man is so brave that he is not disturbed by something unexpected.*

Light and shadow mixed upon the new man's face like military camouflage, his features distorted because of it. For that *he* threw the door down the stairs and returned for the other two, then put some clothes in a bag and headed out into early morning as *his* mother kept repeating*:* "Oh, my god. Oh, my god…"

I walked to my grandparents' house. It was too early to knock, so I sat with my back to a wall and knees to my chest in the tiny porch until my Gran woke in the morning. By the time my gran answered the door *he* had long gone, and I was left to pick up the pieces.

I went to live almost permanently with my grandparents. I had my own room. It was there that *we* felt safest. It also meant that *we* could move to new places and when it was time to leave that place, *we* would just return to *our* grandparents' house.

There was no trouble. No strife. I was always accepted there, which is what made it so appealing. I remember coming home from a trip once and made the mistake of going to my mother's house first. It was an obvious mistake, but I was so tired. I was told I could sleep a couple of hours, but I had to be gone by the time the now older man got in from work.

Gary Troia

Part 2

Gary Troia

Chapter 6

A man only begins to be a man when he ceases to whine and revile, and commences to search for the hidden justice which regulates his life.

James Allen

Maybe the worst thing about going to a new building site was the apprehension the day before. Having to look at an *A to Z of London* to plan the route by train and tube. Then *that* feeling takes hold. Agitation and turmoil tumbling together in the pit of my stomach, knowing I must go where I do not want to be and do what I do not want to do and I've no idea how the transport connections work, so I leave earlier than necessary, which often ends with me standing outside a building site in the dark before the gates are open, alone with my thoughts and tools.

The night before is spent tossing and turning. My alarm clock was big and brassy and made such a racket on each movement of a second that it was a precursor, a constant countdown to when the torture really starts. Mind pain, when it turns up, only exacerbates the situation as I become aware that defiance and resistance towards building sites has at last succumbed to desperation for money. Even though excuses and diversions win far more than they lose, it's no consolation when you're stony-faced on a tube with a bag of tools and heading for a lost day in perdition.

The clothes I wear are shabby: cement-covered jeans, beat up boots, heavy coats. Should I take sandwiches? Is there going to be a canteen or shops nearby? Have I got enough cash for the fare? Cigarettes? Will I take joints or see how it goes first?

I've arrived. Now I'm where I don't want to be. I see the kind of job it is. I am told where to go. I might climb a ladder up a scaffold, or down into a trench to build footings in thick, sticky mud. I take up my position. Take out my trowel and wire brush. Scrape the old mortar off. Here comes the hod carrier, and here come nine hours queuing up, each one pounding their fists together and demanding a brawl before I can be free again.

I look to the heavens to gauge the weather. I might look at cars or buildings, people strolling by, and not one of them are on this site – and I wish I were one of them – anyone of them. But I need money, and before I can get any, I must work two weeks in hand. I don't know what I've done wrong. And worst of all, I don't know how to change it. This is my *Gulag Archipelago*. I've been alone with these thoughts for so long, and I wish more than anything for someone wise to confide in - talk things through, sit me down and tell me where I'm going wrong.

I do not know how many versions went through this first day of horror, but every time it was the same, unless mind pain was upon one of them, then it was worse. If I had been working for a while, and mind pain arrived, then I just didn't bother going in, but if I was at the start of accumulating money, and I had left it a bit late in getting a job – on the edge, so to speak, I would have no option but suffer the mind pain on top of the usual discomfort of starting out on site.

There must be others with mind pain in other tough jobs, I know nothing of them or their minds, but I stand in solidarity with them.

When I remember characters I've met or seen on site, it still shocks me to the core. On one refurbishment job on an office block in London, we were building dividing walls. It was so dark inside that the lead of light bulbs almost never had enough slack to get the light where you needed it. I was working with a Glaswegian. He had Tenants Super lager in his bag. He was always early, and when I got up on the scaffold, before the muck (mortar) had arrived, he had *The Times* newspaper folded on yesterday's hardened brickwork, doing the crossword while gulping generously from a can. He usually finished the crossword before the muck arrived. He was obviously an intelligent man, but how did he end up like he did? Another character I remember was a man in his forties with hardly any teeth. Time had not only caught up with him sooner than it should have, it had overtaken him, and left him lagging way behind in the distance, like a spent marathon runner.

All I ever thought about was not doing brickwork. On one side there was the detestation of building sites and on the other was a feeling of stupidity in not knowing what to do instead. I wanted to write but did not know how to when faced with a blank page, so I just wrote *A Bricklayer's Tales* over and over. At least I had a title. I also had the obstacle of hardly ever going to school and therefore had near to non-existent writing skills.

How many people love their jobs? I would say about two in every hundred, and after that it is just a matter of general satisfaction until you reach the "I hate my job" group. With clearer eyes and a little wisdom, I see that the more I hated my work was when I thought about it the most, and these thoughts bound me tighter to it.

This was my problem. When I was at work, I wanted to be somewhere else, and when I was at home, I was thinking about being at work the next day – and not just the next day - all my working days. I thought of almost nothing other than doing brickwork or avoiding brickwork.

I hardly talk about bricklaying anymore because it brings back bad memories and anxious feelings, but there was one night when the feeling catapulted me way beyond the normal levels of agitation of feeling trapped.

Once when out with friends who had a mixture of jobs, I was subdued as I listed each one's job in my mind and concluded that my plight was the worst of all. The conversation was light and lively, and I became conspicuous by my brooding silence.

It got so bad that I went outside for air, and while outside, I got a cab home and poured drink after drink, rolled joint after joint as I couldn't prevent my mind from attacking itself. It was the first time I realised what Nikos Kazantzakis meant in his prologue to *The Last Temptation* about warring factions of the Evil One and God clashing within his soul, and there was a literal civil war raging in my mind and soul. And now I knew why that passage of his had affected me so much.

The phone kept ringing. It had to be my friends trying

to find out what happened to me. I ignored it at first and turned it off next. Through the window the red neon cross on the church opposite my bedroom mocked me, and if I knew a way of destroying it without having to leave the house, I would have.

The moment arrived where drink and drugs laid me down. I put my headphones on and tried to get my mind to follow the music and forget myself. I knew my mind liked music, so I took care to play some of its favourites.

I drifted off. I dreamed I was living in a bedsit. I could see everything in sharp detail. It was even sharper in my mind than the bedroom would have been had I opened my eyes and looked. I was older. I was alone. And...

I'm looking at my face in a mirror and assure myself it doesn't look as bad as most my age. I spit into a sink and watch the blood from my gums mingled with toothpaste, swirling down the plughole. It's cold.

And it's nearly Christmas.

I'm working on a large refurbishment job by the Thames, so it's even colder there. Fuck it! I am short on t–shirts. I'm going to have to rummage around the laundry basket and sniff out the least offensive. When I say laundry basket, I mean the pile of shit on the floor that represents a laundry basket. I look at this festering pile and assume that the top two are the best bet. I tentatively sniff them, hoping for a result. It's not pleasant, but I slip both on anyhow, focusing the antiperspirant mainly at my arm pits. I splash my face with water (what my Gran would have called a cat's lick) and have a piss. I pull on my work jeans, which have a carboard-like stiff feel to them: lifeless and embedded with mortar from the past couple of weeks. The right-hand pocket is hanging off my anorak. Then my old boots. It's an effort. The blood rushes to my head as I bend to put them on. The right one has a hole in it that lets in water. I drag my hand across my face with a tired sigh. My weekly travel-pass is by the side of my portable TV on the tatty yellow Formica table.

Also on the table are a wine bottle, ashtray, tumbler

and multi–vitamins. Two empty bottles of wine are on the floor. The ashtray is overflowing. A half-smoked joint has fallen out. The thought of drinking and smoking brings instant watery bile to my mouth. It keeps on coming. I keep on swallowing. Soon enough the uprising of bile begins to relent. Finally, I can swallow alcohol and inhale smoke. I heave continuously as I descend the uncarpeted stairs.

I open the door. An icy blast hit me hard. I walk to the train station wondering how much of a future remains to me but get distracted by a crisp packet whipped up by the wind.

When I got home yesterday there was a letter waiting for me. Margaret (the landlady) had placed it on the uncarpeted fourth step as she always does with my mail. I've been receiving a lot of mail recently, mostly from my doctor and the hospital. I can't deal with opening it. I pick it up and put it in my still-attached anorak pocket.

We're pulling into Charing Cross station. I get a cup of coffee from McDonalds. The station clock says that I have time to nip outside and drink it along with smoking one or two cigarettes before I descend the stairs to the District Line. I think of the letter. I think of my age. I think of the past. I think what could have been if only I'd thought differently. The tube-train rattles on. I think about where I'm working: a huge office block that a bank is renovating. The bricklaying foreman calls himself the Viking. He is an absolute cunt, nothing like a Viking - at least nothing like how I imagine a Viking to be. He's even written Viking on his hard hat with a magic marker. I think of my bag of tools, the tools of my trade. Rusty tools. I never clean my trowel properly at the end of the working day. I just slam it edgeways into the spot board two or three times to get rid of most of the muck.

I'm walking over Tower Bridge. I can't remember it being colder this year, but I could be wrong. I protect one hand in my good anorak pocket, the other rests on the torn seam taking the brunt of winter. A clock on one of the buildings I'm walking towards tells me I have time for a cup of tea before I start. I hold the tea tightly with my cold hand. I sit at one of the long benches in the canteen. I close my eyes as the world starts to spin. I can't face the thought of talking to anyone, so I take my tea to the sixth floor. I place it by a concrete column then fetch my tools from under a sheet of insulation where I hid them yesterday.

I lean on a horizontal scaffold tube that stops workers from falling off the building. I look at boats on the Thames bobbing around. I imagine myself on one of them looking at me. The muck is already on my spot board. The labourers get in half an hour before the brickies to ensure there will be no hanging about. My cheeks are stinging from the steely wind. I take the trowel out of my bag and scrape the remaining muck off that wasn't expelled when I hit it on the board yesterday. I'm already four courses up, which is good, as the blood would rush to my head if I had to start from the concrete. I start three minutes early. I hear the Viking walking up the stairs. I anticipate what's coming. He emerges onto the floor I'm working on and shouts out in mock humour, whilst holding his stomach with one hand and tapping his watch with the other: "Look out!" He shouts below, "He's only fucking working and it's not even 'alf – past," still tapping his watch.

I ignore him. When he is far enough away, I close my eyes and reach within and embrace my soul in atonement. I sense it withdraw to the boat I was looking at. Telepathically I send out "goodbye' and telepathically receive "goodbye."

Every time I bend to take the muck from the board, my head begins to pound and the pain increases. I roll the mortar on the board, then work it around the pier I'm building. I take a brick from the stack and ease it gently down. The excess muck, which squeezes out, is scraped off to be used for the perp joint on the next brick. This procedure is repeated continuously until the working day is done.

I assume an hour must have passed, but it hasn't, the clock on an adjacent building tells me thirty-two minutes have. I decide to do another ten minutes and then go to the toilet. I don't want to use the toilet - I just need to sit down.

I remember the letter. I feel for it in my pocket and

touch something else that seems like a joint. It is! I light it and read the letter. It says I've got inoperable, stage four pancreatic cancer. I smile for the first time that day, finish the joint, open the door and look at myself in the plastic mirror.

As I descend the stairs, I hear a commotion going on. I look round the corner of the stair well and see the Viking with his trusted lieutenants, Dave the head hoddy, and Bret the charge–hand. As I stand and look at them, everything so loud and monotonous, I've had enough.

The Viking is standing behind Dave doing a doggy-style movement with everyone standing around laughing. Without a thought to what I'm doing, I start jogging towards them. I'm picking up speed and laughing like a mental case. Dave is the first to notice. He turns his head whilst still being shagged from behind. The Viking stops his pretend shagging and stares. They seem to be standing in awe, as the running man, without a soul, just the husk of a body functioning solely on muscle memory, gains on them quickly.

There is a gap between the scaffolding and the hoist. I focus on the gap before realising that I am now airborne. I manage, with consummate ease, like an Olympic gymnast, a 180-degree turn and see the faces of Dave, Bret and the Viking, with their mouths open, while mine is smiling. I feel like I am standing on a plinth of air, suspended for what seems like an inordinate amount of time until, imperceptibly at first, I begin the descent. To me it feels I'm going the way of the twin towers, not over and twisting, but straight down, feet first, in perfect alignment, finally free.

From the boat, I witness the body falling from the building site. I notice too, a letter fluttering above it. I watch it fall gently into the Thames.

I awake. Sweat dripping from every pore. It took time before I realised I'm not yet the character dreamed about.

It was a few hours before I needed to get up for work, but I already knew I was about to take my leave from this present site. My plan of action seemed to be known before I thought about it. I was going to take time off work – a long time, and that thought settled me, and I was going to think things through. However, I remembered it was Friday so I would go in and collect my cheque first. I was also low on dope and calculated the earliest time I could get some more.

Gary Troia

Chapter 7

Almost three months of laying bricks. There was plenty of work about so the day rate was high. I had more than enough money in the bank not to worry for a while. Another bricky and I were on the line together. He asked if I fancied a pint at lunch. I knew immediately that this job was over. We stayed in the pub until 5 pm and got a cab home. I felt as good as a prisoner on release day.

That night at a local pub, I saw a dealer and bought some cocaine. I snorted a line in the toilet. It was good, removing all thoughts of the grind. There was an isolated bench by a window, so I moved there, staring through the window while my mind raced away with itself, feeling glorious that I couldn't concentrate on any one subject for too long. My perception of time altered. Hours became minutes, whereas on the building site that morning, seconds stumbled by like paralytic units of time.

A familiar voice cut through the crackling in my head as it called my name. I turned to see two men I knew well but hadn't seen for a while. They sat down and after a drink asked me if I wanted to go to Spain the following week as someone had dropped out. I agreed. These two would not have been my first choice travelling companions, yet any chance to get away from where I was will always get my vote. What I didn't like about these two were that they were pretentious and arrogant, looking down on everyone and talking behind everyone's back, especially mine when I was not about. They were cowards of a type, but they knew how to do well in a worldly sense. But I always said to myself after being with them, "what I wouldn't give for their problems without having to be them".

As soon as we got in the hotel room in Spain, they were laying out their clothes and talking about what went with what. I went to the bar. I met a group of Glaswegians and went out with them. The following day I was exclusively hanging out with them.

When the holiday was over the Glaswegians used to phone me on a Friday evening before they went out. Soon they invited me to Glasgow for weekends. I was itching to get away from my place so I asked one of them, whose father was a bricklayer, if he could get me a job.

He came back with a yes and soon I was on a coach to Glasgow with a big bag. Like almost every time, getting away from home was exciting and new and the real me was in charge and happy. But soon the effect of bricklaying wore the situation down to it being just like anywhere. From Glasgow I went with a team to the Shetland Isles to work. We got in a fight, and I was glassed in the hand because the local males didn't take kindly to Glaswegians and a Londoner talking to *their* women. I had stitches in the palm of my hand, so I caught a ride with two carpenters back to Glasgow in their van. It was winter. The snow was falling, and Glasgow seemed bleak. I decided to return to London, which was just as bleak.

The problem when escaping hometown familiarity is that you haven't escaped yourself, and it always catches up with you before too long. If I want to live in a new place, I must get work, so I end up laying bricks in the new place. And there I am again, laying bricks in a new town and the feeling of being in a new town soon becomes as familiar as the old town.

This was a classic trap for versions and something that one of them had to learn to escape from. An opportunity would come over the hill. And it was exciting watching it come. I would be grateful and feel happy. Meeting new people enabled me to be who I wanted to be, but mind pain would come and although I tried to hide it from these new people, eventually I would succumb to cutting myself off and isolate as each version knew so well. Then I would go back to London and hide away because it's easier to hide in such a sprawling mass, and then wait for something to come over the hill again. And it always came.

I Return to Versions of Myself

Chapter 8

He who conquers his spirit is mightier than he that taketh a

city.

Proverbs xxi. 32

I once met two bricklayers on a site that led to long-lasting friendships. I got to know their families and often stayed over at their homes to drink, smoke drugs, go to the pub, and listen to music. I noted that neither of them seemed to harbour any dreams or goals, which seemed to make them content, and they never mentioned that they disliked bricklaying in any way or wanted to do anything different.

I wondered whether a family life and I were compatible. I considered it and concluded that it wasn't. To put myself in their family shoes seemed impossible to my mind. So many versions have often walked streets, thinking, "How do these people live like this? How do they manage and cope with the monotony of everyday life"? Domiciled, going to work, living as a unit, visiting other units be they family or friends, cleaning the car on a Sunday morning - routine. Being responsible for others was the main problem, as I had yet to get close to being responsible for myself, as my mind was, for the most part, a perpetual battleground for control of my mind. Not only that, but what would happen to my family when mind pain came? I would have to go to a room and be left alone with my medicine until it passed. No one wants to put up with that as I had already found from experience. All these were heavy attachments that would have sunk any version without trace if one of them had dared to volunteer to withstand the weight of an accumulation of people, and *things* that lead to weighty responsibility.

Both bricklayers lived on the east side of the Thames, so it was good to frolic there as no one knew me apart from them, allowing me space and freedom to experiment with different outlooks and attitudes.

Although I'd concluded that I could never be responsible enough, owing to a crew of misfits in my mind, still I yearned for what they had: a home and a family. When I left to go home after a night or two, I felt a sudden drop in vibration, a lack of energy. The thought of returning to an empty flat didn't appeal because I realised that I was so far behind *normal* people that if we were back in time, living in small groups, I would probably be an outcast, not in the sense of being banished, but more to do with me not being able to tow the appropriate line. Aquatically I was resigned to being a creature that dwells in a different part of the river. I had no idea how to swim the divide. A home and a family were something that took great effort and patience, and I was mainly irresponsible from a lack of direction and discipline allied to mind pain and other issues. The main fear each version carried was not to be the one that landed *us* on the streets or in jail, which was always the tacit command.

On returning to my flat that housed nothing but the screaming emptiness of nothing, it dawned on me that what was *outside* seemed reminiscent of my *inside* attitude. In one way it was a massive revelation, which quickly switched to me thinking that I might be ill. To counter that, a part of me held the position that I was on a spiritual journey. I could not deny that I was on a journey. Spiritual was debatable; it was more likely to be a nihilistic path to nowhere and nothing, as all the signs were intimating.

I carried on…

Once a month, my two bricklaying companions and I went out after work. We would choose a destination and take a change of clothes, drinks, drugs, and some deodorant to work. I remember the day we went to the Hard Rock Café in London.

It was a different day at work. Like the last day before Christmas or a holiday. The day dragged. Looking at a watch or asking the time resulted in the answer thudding to the floor like a medicine ball, as time moved slowly, much slower even than an everyday workday. When the day ended, I was relieved.

In the canteen we opened beers, chopped lines of coke, and rolled joints. Got changed. Felt better.

We had a couple of pints in a local pub then headed

off. It wasn't just the coke and the drink; we were all in good spirits. Not high spirits, but good spirits. We were laughing and joking, energy up as we entered the Hard Rock Café. At a table across from us were five American girls. We got talking. I had one of their numbers by the end of the evening.

I started to show her around London, even taking her home to my mum's for Sunday lunch. When she left, we kept in touch by letter. The unbridled joy that rose in me on receiving her letters was so joyful that I felt every atom within me vibrating at an optimal level, and only unrestrained joy can make that happen. The letters were long and contained music she'd recorded. This was the first happy mail I'd received since the coded letters back in junior school. To this day I regret the dying art of letter writing. Almost no communication is as personal or as close as a hand-written, well thought out letter.

I felt change. Energy lifted and raised me from my usual humdrum existence. And because I felt change, everything seemed to change around me because I focused on better things. My thoughts were higher, happier, hopeful, and the more they became that way, the more everything increased in that way.

I stopped doing the usual things. I stopped seeing the same old people and changed some negative and habitual practices.

She eventually invited me out to America. I knew she had a boyfriend where I was going to stay. Winter passed. Spring arrived. I was waiting for summer.

I had direction. Everyone needs somewhere to aim for. I started doing overtime. Saved as much as I could. Stopped going out. Felt happier in my mind. Some demons withered and died through lack of attention as the real *me* emerged again to steer the ship and set the course.

To be *authentic* again is what every version lived for and longed always to be…nothing more than that.

I used to sit at home in the evening and think how great it was to be *me* again. And as I settled back into the position of captaining my ship, I began to become aware that I was naturally thinking and acting differently. But to do that, one needs a vision of what to become.

I've mentioned that there was no guide, no one to show me how to navigate my ship. So instead of looking for a role model, I chose my father as an anti-role model, thus abandoning everything he did and do the opposite. At first it seemed a good idea, but soon I saw that I was more of a distorted reflection of him, having not taken on board womanising and gambling, I had taken on drugs, drink and solitude. I got rid of that idea, as I wanted nothing in common with my father, not even the uncommon.

This realisation took me back and I wondered how I could have been so stupid. I carried this thought around until one day I was walking through the local park, and my mind cleared. I saw that the reason my father did what he did was because he had no values and no goals. The only thing he was interested in was chasing women and betting his life away. I've since heard that he was quite good at the first and useless at the second.

He was just a punter who was ultimately a loser, and even in the first of his interests he only ever lost. I learnt that he much regretted it later when living with his last woman on this earth, who he had to keep on good terms with as there would be no other chance at finding someone that would put up with him because he had also lost his looks, which is a devastating blow for a ladies' man.

I Return to Versions of Myself

Gary Troia

Chapter 9

*Reality doesn't impress me. I only believe in intoxication, in
ecstasy, and when ordinary life shackles me, I escape, one way
or another. No more walls.*

Anaïs Nin

I disarm the large brass alarm clock before it has a
chance to be discordant. Countless times I've left my
gran's for work, but not this morning. For a few
seconds I gather up thoughts like an autumn leaf clear
up. An epic smile deploys. "Today I'm flying to the
U.S.", I tell myself. But I rest that thought for a
moment because I want to indulge myself in
imagining where I'm not going: a building site. It's
hard to hold the excitement of what's ahead - it's
delayed gratification, and I've read somewhere that
delayed gratification is a wise decision that will yield
benefits somewhere down the line.

The church opposite is muted in the fading dark of
morning's arrival. Only at night when the red neon

cross blazes does it have any power.

Happiness is revving my engine. I'm licking metaphorical lips in anticipation of an unknown world to come. I try to tamp it down. I scan the bedroom. It looks old. It has no sense of being a refuge today, more of a nest that a fledgling is about to take a leap of faith from.

I pick up a half-smoked joint in the ashtray to toast the unchartered river that will carry me far from here, beyond familiar haunts into virgin territory.

I hear the voice of my gran downstairs. She has made tea and Marmite on toast. She is smiling as I eat and drink. A single tear rolls down her cheek. She wipes it dry. I return to my bedroom.

In the dirty laundry basket are working jeans, t-shirts, socks, etc. But before I throw them in a bin bag, I stop and reacquaint myself with the dry, dusty aroma of cement and sand. A puff of dust plumes up as tiny particles swirl in the thin sunlight.

After saying goodbye to my gran, she calls after me,

"When will we see you again"?

I have no idea. I hadn't thought about it.

"Soon", I replied. "Soon".

I wave and make my way to the tower block. Why am I going there? I go to clarify what I'm leaving behind. A flat of joints smoked, drinks drunk, and fights won and lost, and where I waited, often in vain, for something to come over the hill. I get one good piece of advice from one of them: "If you feel bad, just remember that". He was pointing twenty floors below at the drab grey scene full of narrow brick council houses and tower blocks. A farewell joint as a peace pipe is smoked.

I'm waiting at the train station to go to Heathrow airport. The joints given me an edgy feel at the thought of what lies ahead today, blood sloshing side to side in my brain, feeling like a man in a small boat in choppy water, about to lose sight of a familiar shoreline.

At Heathrow I wait in the departure lounge, checking

out a row of British Airways 747s staring back at me through vast windows. I need a big plane to make a big change.

Excess energy is pulsing through my body. I feel cast adrift. Maybe this is what Kierkegaard meant when he wrote "Anxiety is the dizziness of freedom". I am entirely free, or seemingly so outwardly, because along with me board a disparate, unseen crew of demons, attitudes, misplaced pride, anger, guilt, self-pity, and a captain who is often missing in action, usually to be found drunk in his cabin; and not forgetting mind pain that comes and goes as it pleases. But here we go, nevertheless.

Ideas feed and flood my imagination. I have flown countless times, but this is different. It's not Spain for a two-week package deal. I have no comprehension of what's coming my way. I enter *my* mind that is mostly empty but for expectation and a made-up story of the future.

I'm leaving behind family and friends, the majority of whom don't even know I'm leaving. Apart from my grandparents and the acquaintances in the tower block, I've told almost no one. I have no home but a room in my grandparents' house. I have no car because I never have anywhere to drive to. I've got cash and a journey mapped out in front of me, and that is all I need.

On the plane I set in motion a sequence of thoughts that lead me to envisage myself as anyone I want to be. The realisation that it is possible to be who I want to be is laid at my feet as an offering.

Take off feels like a sudden reduction of weight being left behind as I'm launched through London's grey cloud. Ahead of me waits an American girl and America. I can't help but create exceptional thoughts. They start like a trickle through a tiny fissure in my mind before breaking out from every direction. I ask for a gin and tonic even though I've never had one before.

For the first time in the life of any version comes a barrage of self-reflection that had never been unearthed, never been examined. My mind is flowing free like a torrent of water from a burst bank, splashing creative ideas onto an abstract riverbank of possibilities. I want to forget everything I know and become brand new. I want to make new memories, as most of my memories are a dirge of sadness and hopelessness. I want more than anything to be free from them...

I see that jumbo jet flying over the Atlantic now. I see that version sitting by the window. I sense the vibration of thought flowing through his mind. But although the idea of escaping building sites makes him happy, he is unaware that he is not escaping himself.

His euphoria cannot be sustained. I wish I could tell him to visualise a higher set of values to live by. But even if I could sit beside him on that plane, a sedate and serious talk would not reach through his euphoric high.

That version, fizzing with apparent change, is far from ready. For him the sun is shining. It is warm, but soon the winds of mind pain will whistle through broken windows and empty streets that will make him reach out for help from demons to retake the helm when those pitiless winds inevitably start to blow. It is right that a version looks ahead to the fruits of a goal, but the real skill is being prepared for it before it arrives. I have been familiar with versions who have thought correctly but received what they wanted too soon.

He is naïve, of course, but also unequalled in satisfaction, so let's not take that away from him. We will leave him on that plane over the Atlantic to enjoy his euphoria, because God knows it won't last.

I bound through customs aware of how good I feel. No matter what I think about, no matter the aspect, position, whatever I look upon, my life is in shape as reflected in everything I see.

…I catch a glimpse of myself in a mirrored column: I'm looking good. My hair is well cut, shaved from the neck, cut in layers. I'm wearing light-blue jeans and a dark bluish-purple jacket with thin black stripes running through it. I ask myself if I've ever looked better, and the answer is "unlikely". I sweep on and look forward to meeting the American girl.

I ask myself questions: Is my bank account in good order? I smile before I answer. Am I nervous about meeting her again? No. Am I worried that she won't be waiting? No. I look for a scenario that might throw me. There isn't one.

As I'm about to emerge into arrivals, I do have a question that I don't know the answer to: Why can't I be like this all the time?

Right now, regret and guilt are unknown to me.

My body is in shape and letting me know that it is in shape. There are no niggles or pain bothering me. It comes to mind that this is how Jesus might have felt: in complete harmony with everything; neither superior nor diminished, powerful, fearless, and at peace.

The American girl is standing with her boyfriend and another girl. A true smile lifts and separates my lips because I am authentic.

Out on the road the smell is different. The two girls are in the back. Still smiling as I look out at different houses and different advertisements. This is a foreign country that speaks English. The girl unknown to me in the back asks to touch my hair. I say no. She touches my hair.

I've often heard it said that everything in America is bigger. I saw it as wider, which is bigger, so maybe I mean more spacious. Land is at a premium in Britain. There's not much of it in comparison.

At a party that night I get talking with the other girl. We are attracted to each other in a way that is different to any girl I've ever met. More connected. Deeper. The next few days are spent sitting at the home of the girl I met in the Hard Rock café in London. Sometimes I ride into D.C. with her, or just sit on the grass outside the house and read books; the constant buzz of crickets is unrelenting. I think often of the other girl, Claudia. I'm eager to see her, but she has gone to Los Angeles with her mother for a funeral.

Gary Troia

Chapter 10

Watch your mind carefully for any beliefs that hinder its
accomplishment, and step away from them.

A Course in Miracles

A red-carpet experience comes over the hill and rolls gently down with so much script already woven into it that all any version must do is play a part; but a valuable lesson learned by a recent version was that you had better have another plan formulated for when the carpet runs out.

Almost everything bowed to my favour. Nothing was forced or manipulated. It was like acting in a play where everyone's part is written but mine.

Days vanished sitting on the lawn outside listening to the crickets as I read books or wandered around the local area. I visited the Smithsonian, had lunch in a bar, or just ambled about. I felt free and everything seemed brand new. Often, I thought of Claudia who was still in Los Angeles with her mother. Days later a postcard arrived from Los Angeles, and I was mentioned, she hoped I was having a good time. Although it was addressed to the girl I met in London, I knew that the actual content was meant for me. When she returned, Claudia phoned and asked me out. She turned up a couple of hours later in her car. From that moment on we became inseparable and almost before I knew it, I had moved in with her.

My holiday had now turned into something else. I naïvely phoned the American immigration department and asked if I could work for six months. I continued to think about employment and staying on as I felt comfortable and kept reminding myself of the view from the tower block in southeast London. I came across a newspaper that was the equivalent of the *London Evening Standard*. Under the job section there was a lot of work on offer but no bricklaying jobs. I started alphabetically and learned that bricklayers in this part of the U.S. are called masons. I called one. My heart beat a quick rhythm waiting for someone to answer. I asked for a job and the woman said yes. She said that the foreman would be pleased to meet me as he was from Liverpool. I got the address and started the following morning.

It was a huge site. I had difficulties with measurements because they used imperial whereas Britain uses the metric system. I was excited for the first time in my life at the prospect of going to a building site. But at the end of the first day the foreman came to me and said he couldn't keep me on as it was a government job, and I couldn't be paid cash in hand. I was devastated but he paid me for the day and wished me well.

I was undeterred. I kept ringing and soon got another job. This time I told them that I didn't have a green card and they said it didn't matter. There was a building boom and cash in hand was not a problem for them.

There was plenty of work and, even though it was brickwork, I felt grateful. But as the weeks went on, the feeling of gratitude drifted away and was replaced with an aching sense of drudgery. I started to find work hard. As I trimmed a brick with the edge of my trowel, a small, sharp piece hit me in the corner of my left eye. I blinked a few times as this can often dislodge it, but not this time. In the toilet I pulled my eyelids apart and saw the fragment. Dabbing my eye with tissue did the trick. The drab container where we ate our lunch and got changed was like all building site containers, dusty and uncomfortable. Outside I saw the mixer turning relentlessly before I became aware of the whirring sound it made. The scaffold to build a chimney was being erected. Me and another brickie were going to build it. Although I had built a few chimneys, this one seemed higher and more dangerous. I felt the tension in my mind spread to the rest of my body before my mind started to find excuses to get away. I felt foreign as I heard two Americans talking. I was foreign. I was hesitant to go back to work as my anxiety would show. Where was the authentic me?

The energy that I once had dropped to an unhelpful low, and soon I saw the site I was working on as the same as any old site back home, or anywhere in the world. The nightmare returned and mind pain emerged for the first time on the American continent, so I had to revert to well-worn techniques to cope with ordinary, everyday situations. I returned to drink and drugs. That afternoon I managed to persuade the work crew that a trip to the bar at lunch time would make a welcome change. I got through as many as I could in the available time.

Gary Troia

Chapter 11

Henceforth I travel toward Repose
The Gospel of Mary Magdalene

Back in England, a flat I'd bought off plan, had been completed, so I decided to go back and sell it. This was a blessing – not just for the money that was coming my way – but it was a chance to get home and recuperate before mind pain caused me to buckle mentally and behave badly. I told Claudia that I would buy her a ticket when the flat was sold. She was excited by that and looked forward to visiting England. I had saved a fair amount and was relieved that I wouldn't have to work while home and I could also afford to pay the mortgage until the flat was sold.

At first it was such a relief to be home. The tension that almost overwhelmed me began to dissipate, and I was pleased that I had not let myself down in the eyes of Claudia and the New World, which had been a close call.

I gradually began to regain a semblance of authenticity. I became a poor man's raconteur with my tales of travel and my new foreign girlfriend. It was like being back at primary school when I was an explorer bringing pomegranates, but this time it wasn't exotic fruit I bore, but an exotic woman.

The flat sold and made a healthy bank account. It felt good buying Claudia a ticket to London. Her mother and sister took her to the airport and the ticket was waiting for her. The following day I asked her to marry me, which seemed to take me by surprise more than her.

At the time I had strange ideas about many things and one of them was that two people should get married for themselves and not be a spectacle for others, so we just had two witnesses; my mother sat in a car outside the registry office with her friend like MI5 surveillance operatives.

We stayed in England for a couple of months before returning to my new home. I was sure that a new life away from the old one would change everything for the better, but although the red carpet had yet to run out, I was getting close to the end without any plan of what to do next, or any kind of awareness about minimising and coping with the effects of mind pain. At Heathrow I was not alone - I had a wife, and for the first time I realised that I had a massive responsibility. The raconteur and all his amusing stories were just a theatrical memory, now came reality and obligations, although I consoled myself knowing I had eight hours on a plane to think and drink about it.

Gary Troia

Chapter 12

God laid down this law, saying: if you want some good, get it from yourself.

Epictetus

Day-to-day living soon took the gloss off and my new life was no longer brand new, so when mind pain came, it was always like an unprovoked attack from a violent foe. I knew nothing about mental health then and so I couldn't, even if I wanted to, explain it to my wife.

Never in my life had I spoken deeply with anyone about anything that mattered. Neither family, friends, nor girlfriends, not even with doctors or counsellors. The pain and tension I carried with me was something I thought I would grow out of sooner or later. It was now later, and nothing had changed. Just like always, opportunities arrived, and then departed. Yet I never considered that opportunities would come to an end.

For a year and a half, we lived in an apartment. I continued to work on building sites, and Claudia managed a restaurant in the evenings. Our workday hours hardly ever coincided. Sometimes I was up and loving life, full of confidence, but with no foundation to hold the confidence up, and mind-pain all the while was patiently waiting to bring my structure down.

One day I returned to our apartment and immediately noticed there were fewer items in it. Claudia had taken her things.

I had made enough money to see out the storm in my mind, and although I was devastated that she had gone, another part was relieved to be alone to recuperate. We terminated our contract on the condo, giving me a month to find somewhere new. As we left the office, I saw sadness in her eyes that her choice of husband had been unwise. I just wanted to get in and close the door on *out there,* looking forward to the cache of drink and drugs that were waiting to console and wrap their faithful arms around me.

I Return to Versions of Myself

Gary Troia

Chapter 13

Happy is the man who has broken the chains which hurt the mind, and has given up worrying once and for all.

Ovid

I watched her car drive off. I stood there even when it had gone from sight. I saw the swimming pool and relived happy times playing volleyball with neighbours. But I must not recall memories good or bad, I must tend to myself if I have any chance of re-emerging on the surface of life. I walked up the staircase, opened the door and closed it behind me, fastening every available lock. I gave myself two weeks of self-indulgence. Two weeks of taking any medicine I liked without a thought of right or wrong.

The apartment being empty was conducive to my state of feeling, there was no longer electrical entertainment, it was all gone. My inner world was like a primordial soup of a distant planet, and I could not foresee what might emerge from it, so I stood back like a shoddy god and waited to see what happened.

After two weeks of only leaving the apartment to get drink, drugs, and food, I felt well enough to go to a local bar. Ordering a second beer, an English accent said, "Are you English"? We got talking and he mentioned that he knew someone who was looking for a tenant. I moved in that evening. The river of my life snaked in a direction I wasn't expecting, I never saw it coming over the hill, or round the river bend.

I returned to laying bricks...

As time went on, I found out my next-door neighbour was a serious drug dealer. More time vanished before my roommate introduced him to me. He was old school. We hit it off and became close, close enough for me to witness large amounts of weed wrapped in industrial polythene in his basement. I took orbit around his sun. He was discreet, dignified, had a quiet sense of power about him. There was an extensive library in his house, and a telescope in one of the bedrooms, where I spent hours, stoned, looking at the heavens. For the first time in my life, I began to discuss big ideas. I began to think differently. He was like a combination of a father and a teacher, and I often thought if I'd only had a thin sliver of a decent father, how might that have helped?

I began to see him as a mentor. I started to accompany him in his truck wherever he went, as he liked me being around. He told me I was different to his usual associates. We took *merchandise* to his boat and sailed down the local river to a quiet spot where men appeared and moved it from the boat into trucks. I soon had lots of cash in my pocket. I never returned to collect my tools from the site I last worked on, or collected the wages owed to me. I somehow felt noble for not doing that.

I began to feel like someone else. A new version muscled his way in, and this one was confident and brimming with thoughts about aspects of life never contemplated before.

There was a large bar where rag-tag individuals and

groups conglomerated. Although it wasn't a regular haunt, you had to be up for it and on high alert after entering, as things could take a nasty turn from just a wrong look or an innocent remark. One sunny, crisp afternoon on a winter's day, I got into a disagreement with a huge man known for his violent tendencies. It was about American football. The disagreement eventually crossed a Rubicon. I decided impromptu to allow one of my crew to take it forward. I had no idea where it would end, but the disagreement was ended when my *other voice* suddenly said, "I see what you mean. I see your point. I've never thought about it like that. Let me buy you a drink". Although the man was physically threatening, my inner *associate* was mentally threatening in a subtle manner, and the big guy was happy to get out of the argument because he was losing it.

Soon after I started to have dreams about American jails after watching a documentary. One morning I got up and felt differently. My awareness was strong, it overpowered all my flimsy feelings of self-importance and bravado. I thought about the confrontation with the bear in the bar and shook my head at the audacity *I'd* shown. I had lost my appetite for the world of illicit drug deals. I went and explained this to my next-door neighbour. I didn't know if I expected him to smile or not, but he told me that I had made the right decision. He gave me a packet of money and said it was good to know me. I was about to tell him where I was going, but he turned his back, got into his truck and drove off. I felt like a character in a film learning a valuable lesson. I was still sharing a house with two others from the chance meeting with the Englishman from the bar, so I gave them two months' rent. We had a party. Then I got in a car and drove a long way from that place. Sometimes I wonder what happened to my brief mentor and feel somewhat nostalgic for that slice of time. I also knew that for once, I had timed an ending of a chapter with consummate precision.

I got work bricklaying again and found a small apartment, and so a new version introduced himself on the first page of a new chapter.

Gary Troia

Chapter 14

We must be willing to let go of the life we have planned, so as to accept the life that is waiting for us.

Joseph Campbell

When mind pain comes, the best solution I found was to isolate and have the least interaction with the world as possible, ideally none. Space to be when not beholden to money is worth far more than money itself. When mind pain rampages at its worst, it lays me low like a heavyweight champion's punch, and there is nothing I can do about that. I sometimes wondered if there were ever a fire or some other serious problem, would I have the will or motivation to get up and move, or prefer to take the consequences that I see unfolding? Just waiting to be consumed, crushed, or carried away. I consider mind pain like a coming tempest; it is pointless to run outside and shake a fist at it to make it stop, turn direction or beg for special dispensation. But this is what I'd done in the past when it threatened, futilely attempting to fight it back and beat it into submission. On the street with mind pain was a concoction that was dangerous to others and me. I would often get upset or angry with someone for the merest slight.

There's a particular passage written by a world-famous self-help author who wrote that all one needs to do when depressed is to jump about and shout "hallelujah". The word depression, in my opinion, needs to be dropped from the psychological lexicon because its connotations of being miserable, downbeat, moping about, maudlin and morose are forms of low mood, whereas true depression is something far deeper, dangerous, dark, and painful. The phrases "Man up. Cheer up. Pull yourself together", are antiquated phrases from a time when men were men, and these *men* knew nothing of mental illness or what they were talking about. I prefer the term mind pain, because it literally hurts my mind.

I never saw this coming, but my wife and I met up again and got back together. Although born in Brazil, she was brought up in California and wanted to return, so we packed up and drove across the country.

We lived in Long Beach for a while but soon drifted apart once more, and I moved to Venice Beach. It was a crazy place. I lived a block from the beach, and every Saturday I would walk from where I lived down the boardwalk to the end of the line of entertainers. I remember a middle-aged man in red and white stripes and a top hat dancing to a music box on roller skates. It was just like watching a man who had put on skates for the first time. He spent all his time trying not to fall over, and that was his act. I always gave him money; it was like watching a representation of my life that made me want to laugh and cry simultaneously.

The builder I worked for took a few weeks holiday, so I decided to take a few too, and return to England. On my return to the U.S., I decided on a different route back to Los Angeles. I would buy some hash and fly to Washington D.C. and make a present of it to my friend that I once spent so much time with, as he once told me that he'd never tried hash. Then I would get the train to Los Angeles. But my trip never panned out like I imagined. Instead, it went like this:

There is always a first time for everything. This is the first time I've waited to board a plane handcuffed to a sheriff. I don't know if he is an actual sheriff – he may be a deputy, for all I know – but he does have one of those metal star-like badges you see in westerns, I just can't get a proper look at it as the handcuffs prohibit my movement.

I'm sitting in the departure lounge at Baltimore Washington International Airport, and all the adults in the lounge are pretending not to look at the sheriff and me. Their children, however, are still unhampered by social protocol. The parents continually yank their children back from trying to find out what they themselves are dying to know. I feel like shouting "It was only a bit of hash, for fucks sake, I'm quite sure you've all had the odd crafty one?"

Me and the sheriff are last off the bus. We wait whilst everyone else boards the plane. The sheriff hands my passport to the chief purser, unfastens the handcuffs, and then I too board the plane. In my seat I take one last perfunctory look at the land of the free, then slam the plastic shutter down on three years of my life.

There was always a room for me at my gran's house, and after giving her a necessary but unlikely story, I went to my room to lie down. I tried hard to prevent the recent trauma from overwhelming me, but it was hard, too hard. My grandparents decorated this room for me when I was a child, the wallpaper depicted cowboys and Indians, and all I could think was that the cowboys have triumphed again.

Gary Troia

Chapter 15

What we achieve inwardly will change outer reality.

Plutarch

I never wanted the flight back to England to end. I would be happily flying it now (like an old episode of the *Twilight Zone)* if I could have made contact and a pact with supernatural forces, rather than getting off in the morning to face the stark reality that was waiting, because I could already picture with perfect clarity what that was.

It was early morning when we began our approach to Heathrow. The plane descended through an ocean of grey over London; yet I could have been descending through my own mind, such was the vastness of cloud hiding hope.

I disembarked the plane like a stumbling, struggling heavily burdened mule, that came forth through customs into a throng of people on the concourse that were arriving, leaving, waiting, or working. I was struggling to cope with the barbaric enormity of reality at a busy airport. I was a dead-end arrival from *somewhere* going nowhere. I needed directions of what to do next.

I sat on a bench feeling shattered mentally, physically, and spiritually. My mind had not the wherewithal to create a basic plan, and my body would not have responded anyhow. The thought of going *home* a failure was too much to comprehend. I could hear all *their* voices in perfect clarity, singing it like a Welsh Voice choir that only I could hear: "He has fucked it up, he has fucked it up again".

I booked a room in a local hotel for three nights and hunkered down as one would in a frontline ditch in war. With each passing thought the room seemed to expand, or else I was contracting. Everything was big. I was small. Even going out for alcohol seemed like a dangerous mission. I was so sensitive that it hurt when someone even glanced at me. Most versions cope with endings as if they are chapters, but this seemed like the summing up of a book.

And then the panic set in. I stared through the window watching planes take off, remembering the happiness of a recent version with a carefree grin and a gin and tonic in his hand, saying goodbye to London. Now I was back, bumping along like a bottom-feeder eating up old familiar ways, wondering what was wrong with *me*. At times like these I hoped and longed for an asylum – not a grey hospital in a city, but a pretty one like an old chateau in the south of France like where Van Gogh stayed for a while – not the part when he was confined to solitary confinement in a padded cell, but when he shuffled along garden paths muttering to himself. My needs would be satisfied with a small amount of bread, cheese, and red wine, yet unlike him, I would be in no need of an easel or paints.

Nothing would be coming over the hill for an inordinate length of time. I knew that. There wasn't even a hill. A thought came that spawned a colony of thoughts. I had to go back to my grandparents' house. Get a job on a building site, and never meet a woman that I truly loved again. The next woman, if any, would just be another person.

Nietzsche wrote that we live the same life repeatedly, but I seemed to be living the same chapter within a life repeatedly.

A thought broke in about getting a plane somewhere. Where? Anywhere! But my mind could not countenance it, and my body was too weak.

For three days a trial was held in that hotel room. On judgment day the verdict was swift because there was no defence. I had committed a grand crime of wasting a gift from the gods – a red carpet gift, no less. Once I handed down the sentence to myself, I accepted it, which resulted in my dread piping down enough to sleep.

I arrived at my gran's in a black cab, which cost a relative fortune, because the pain and shame of too many eyes on a public transport ride across London would have been too much to bear. The plan was to explain as little to my gran as possible, and then buy drugs and alcohol and sit it out for as long as it took.

The term soul-searching seems like a cliché, so I sought out a better term but kept coming back to it because it was exactly what I was doing. Although I was grateful that I had a room to go to, the wallpaper and the plaster that had blown in places on the walls was a stark reminder of what I had just relinquished in a country where I was no longer welcome, as the stamp in my passport screamed: *Undesirable*! When I looked out the window, I saw my grandparents' narrow southeast London garden, rather than a swimming pool outside an apartment in the U.S.

The wallpaper not only depicted a memory of a child version, but it also reflected the latest version of a child in an adult's body. In many ways the wallpaper was more of a mirror, except the mirror was on four walls, so there was no escaping me, no matter which way I turned.

The version writing this now has tried to think of a particular version that existed for the longest amount of time without transforming – living the longest chapter of hopelessness without growth, and after scrolling through my memory, that was the one, the deported one, sitting in that bedroom, who gave up for the longest time.

It took such a time to get over what had been lost. I was back where I started and could not get the images and memories of frittered away opportunities out of my head. I felt doomed to live in an endless loop of up, down, wait; up, down, wait. During all these chapters every version has looked without and found nothing of any use. I remembered a version that found a key to a hopeful door that led to the realisation that everything *out there* might just be an effect, and you can't expect effects to teach you much, because you need to find the cause. I should have persevered with that idea. I spent the first couple of months in a purgatorial haze, aided and abetted by my lifelong companions, drink and drugs. I only stared into space, or through the window at the church and its red neon cross. It just went on and on like purgatory does, which in many ways is worse than hell itself.

I Return to Versions of Myself

Gary Troia

Chapter 16

You must go on. I can't go on. I'll go on.
Samuel Beckett

Almost every day I heard Pam, the young Jamaican woman next door, come in and talk to my gran. She would stay for tea and a chat. My gran enjoyed her company. When I was in the U.S., they'd become friends. She helped my gran out. I got to know her too, but it took a while of just listening before I could cope with conversation.

She was a churchgoer, and once we got to know each other she started to ask me to come along. Sometimes I used to sit in her house with her and her lodger, Annemarie who also went to the same church. I revelled in our chats about church and religion. Every Sunday morning without fail, Pam and Annemarie would knock on the door and ask my gran if I wanted to go. I used to be in bed with a hangover, thinking, "Why are they so bloody persistent"? But I liked them, so it wasn't an inconvenience. Often, I would be smoking my morning joint when I heard them ask my gran if I wanted to go, and it was always followed by my gran's stock reply: "I don't think so, loves".

Days after leaving the U.S. became months. Time does not heal memories like it heals physical pain but increasing distance from the cause of the memory stretches the pain to a certain point which removes much of the initial sting.

I had more energy but no real joy in anything. Old friends came to ask if I wanted to go out for a drink, but I didn't want to go to a bar like I didn't want to go to church. Apart from my grandmother, Pam, and Annemarie, I spoke with no one else. I had no interest in anything, except taking substances that put me into a familiar place between remembrance and forgetfulness. I was usually quite adept at getting the dosage right. At night I stared at the red neon cross on the church, and it just glowed.

I sat on the edge of the bed, smoked joints and remembered the different mental state of the version that took what he thought was a last look at the cross on the morning of the flight to the U.S. I preferred at night to be awake because almost everyone else was asleep. The daylight brought people out, and the light was too sharp and painful for my senses; the night was friendlier. If I wasn't staring at the red neon cross, it was the stars above it on a clear night. The further away objects were, the better I liked them.

After long enough I felt that tiredness was making efforts at rubbing me out like a misplaced pencil mark. It wasn't the tiredness from the constant use of substances, it was the realisation that if I did not put a time on a release date from my self-imposed sentence, it would become an actual life sentence. "After all", I said to myself: "I'm not that bad. I've just made a lot of stupid mistakes".

I understood that when I was authentic, there were never any issues rattling around *inside* to be dealt with. I was never concerned with anything regarding myself, nor looking for reality to be other than it is, because I was right inside and therefore all was right *out there*, and if I wasn't concerned with me, then there was nothing to be concerned about. That is the beauty of authenticity. But just being a degree out of kilter is where wrong conclusions are drawn, and bad decisions made. They originate and are mistakenly formed by an unhelpful childhood. It might be mature to say, "well, I can't blame my parents", but they must accept some responsibility. And just saying I forgive them may well be wise, but it's not enough for healing to take place. That requires forgiveness - a lot of forgiveness. Not only that but it's not just parents and close family members and friends that have an influence, but those you've never known, born long before you were even thought of, from many years ago that are affecting our minds because their thoughts and ways have accumulated, strengthened and become a part of thinking in the present.

One night I looked at the joint I was smoking and stubbed it out. The sense of relief was immediate. I was still stoned a long time after, but my thinking eventually cleared like clouds puffed away by the wind to leave the sunshine. I looked at my books in the corner. They seemed like apparitions, as they had been seemingly invisible before that moment. The wallpaper seemed different. It belonged to a boy, not to the version sat on the bed with the red neon cross illumined behind him.

The following Sunday, Pam and Annemarie knocked at the door. I was ready and waiting for them. I will never forget the joy and surprise on their faces. On the train to Charing Cross, they kept repeating, "We knew God would work this out". And I thought, "When you have lost sight of hills, and when the land is flat, you take what's on offer".

Gary Troia

Chapter 17

*"Dear God," she prayed, "let me be something every minute of
every hour of my life."*
Betty Smith

The main church meeting was held on a Sunday
morning at the Odeon, Leicester Square where major
films premier.

Before the service, my neighbours took me into
McDonalds for coffee. On almost every table sat a
small group of people, each with a bible, flicking thin
biblical pages back and forth, creating an ethereal
whispery whir. It was plain what was happening.
Church members who had evangelized the previous
week were now going through scripture with their
recently landed fish. I took my coffee outside, lit a
cigarette, and watched the throng interacting.

The service was lively. No tired old churchmen, but a
succession of energetic men and women, some

educated, some not, their zeal carrying them along; yet I had a desire for *it* to end. Putting money into a bag signalled the beginning of the end, and I was glad to give.

When the service was over, most of the congregation milled about outside, the energy still palpable among the flock. I locked eyes with a red head that I instinctively knew I would connect with. It was a recognition, as her essence seemed familiar although our bodies were strangers, a reciprocated knowingness was acknowledged through our eyes.

Back home I said goodbye to the neighbours. They were still smiling. Upstairs in my bedroom I knew two things: I was going to give this a chance because there was much I could learn, but that it would have a foreseeable finish. This was the first time I considered a psychological experiment to see how I would turn out.

I was assigned a family group. One of the leaders took a shine to me and within a short span of time I'd moved into a smart flat with him and another member of the church. I started to go to dinner with various members. One day we went for a drive to Kent so he could minister to one of the flock. It took me by surprise that we went to a veterinary practice run by the red head. She quickly finished stitching up a dog and came upstairs and offered us a drink, (she told me later that she regretted rushing the dog's stitching). I was more than happy to accept a beer and stay. The group leader soon realised that we were enjoying the encounter too much, so I was disgruntled when he concocted a lie about having to visit another member. It was the first time I had evidence that this was going to be just like any other group in the world.

The red headed woman was a South African. I will call her Fiona. Before we spoke to each other it was clear we had already connected outside the cinema in London, but next to her I realised how limited my education was. I felt embarrassed. I was invited to dinner with her friends. I remember sitting in a pub before one dinner, having a pint or two, as I was intimidated by their learning. I sat there thinking that this is another opportunity that has arrived over the hill, but rather than an immediate gift of potential possibility, it was more like a direct road to educational redemption.

At a particular dinner party there was a psychiatrist, a vet, a teacher and a couple of lawyers. Everyone seemed outwardly confident. It took a while for me to get going, and although I hadn't the education or knowledge for references to fall back on when I spoke, I did have innate wit and awareness in my armoury to call upon once I'd settled down. Even so, it was obvious that I was raw and uneducated in comparison. These dinners taught me a valuable lesson that I didn't need to be someone else, all I had to do was open long closed shutters and get serious about removing one bad habit after the next and replacing them with quality to return to authenticity.

We went to art exhibitions and my thirst for knowledge soon became insatiable. One day walking down the Embankment in London, we came across booksellers. There were huge trestles stacked with books. As we started to browse, Fiona began to pick up one book after another until she had an armful. I never thought for a moment when she paid for them that she would give the bag to me. For the first time in my life, I was about to read something other than a bible or a football programme.

I went through that bundle of books in a couple of weeks. I read until my blurred vision put an end to it. I wondered how I'd got so far without reading. Those first few books were kindling that sparked a raging fire within me.

After church one Sunday, I didn't go home with Pam and Annemarie, instead I walked to Charing Cross Road where there were many bookstores. When I look back at that version of me, I can only say, "Bless him". I can see him now, wandering around different sections on different floors, innocently naïve as he thought: "I never knew there were so many books and so many subjects". I remember a couple of early purchases like *The Unbearable Lightness of Being* and *The Last Temptation,* and contemplating whether it was still worthwhile to learn Latin. In my little flat empty shelves became full of words and ideas.

One evening, Fiona said to me: "Why don't you go and study"? I assumed that ship had sailed when I left school. But soon the thought dominated my mind, and I learned there was such a thing as a mature student.

I started an English literature course in the evening after work. We went to see a Shakespeare play, which was my first visit to a theatre. But although I understood the content of the books we read and joined in the debate about them, I had no writing skills, so when the exam results came back, I was the only one of the group who failed. My paper was so bad that it didn't even make the lowest grade. I said to myself on the way home: "This failure will never happen again".

But it hadn't ended in failure because when I came to see it for what it was, when there was time to reflect, I still had taken the course and learned much. I'd opened a door and walked right into a room that used to read: NO ENTRY.

The following year I found a college close to where I

lived that did an access course covering a few subjects. The start was a few months away, and for the first time in my life, I formulated a plan. The first thing I needed to do was gird myself and work without interruption on a site to earn as much as I could. Because the more money I had, the less chance of having to work while studying.

Almost before I knew it there was a healthy bank balance and the course was bounding toward me like a puppy in a park. I felt so good knowing that I had months of nothing but study ahead of me without any money worries. It was a pleasing time of my life. I left the church. I had hoped that I might find an external god in the church, like a father, but found something better, something that could cause actual change: it was an awareness of a latent source of inspiration that existed within me.

It was frowned upon to miss church on a Sunday, but I had planned to be ill and had a friend lined up to move me out after the others in the house had left for church. I had an apartment rented. That night I settled in as my phone kept bleeping and ringing from church members all evening. The following day Fiona turned up unexpectedly. I had shaved my head the previous day to signal a clean break and a new start. She looked shocked. We went for a drink in a local pub. As I was talking to her, I realised that I no longer felt less than. It was the last time I saw her. What I'm about to say doesn't sound particularly thankful, but it's the highest compliment I could bestow on anyone at that time: She was a signpost at a pivotal point in my life, pointing to a path for me to take, and for that I am eternally grateful and indebted to her.

I Return to Versions of Myself

Gary Troia

Chapter 18

Whenever two people meet, there are really six people present.
There is each man as he sees himself, each man as the other
person sees him, and each man as he really is.

William James

I was going in the right direction. Money was in the bank.

I was studying and felt as free and as happy as the primary school swimmer. I studied grammar and memorised dictionary definitions. The old crowd and haunts bored me. I became prudent in my affairs, budgeted, and cut expenditure to the bone for fear of having to go back on site to get some more.

I loved college. Every night before sleep I indulged myself briefly, imagining my life before college - just a thought about it lowered my energy, so I was careful not to indulge too much because a prolonged image of laying bricks on a site was enough to pull me toward a helter-skelter of bad times — and why wouldn't it? Seneca saw that a man can't think of becoming great if it "… involves a bent back and an earthward gaze". I began to understand the massive divide and consequences of useful thinking as opposed to wrong thinking, and what a world of difference there was between the two.

When I enrolled at college, I chose English literature and language as the main course of study, and philosophy and mathematics as interesting additions. It was like I had never heard of education – and in a way I hadn't, but it was more to do with never having experienced it. I was amazed there were courses available for those who'd either failed school or had education pass them by, or just wanted to study because they could.

It was obvious the teacher that took philosophy did not really know much about it. Maybe he'd drawn the short straw in having to deliver it, yet it was in that class where I decided to study it further. He had a copy of Bertrand Russell's *A History of Western Philosophy,* and he called it his bible. Each week he chose a chapter, and we discussed it.

Taking maths was a bit of a struggle, but I tried hard and got a lot out of it. I realised that I could do what once seemed unfathomable to me. I used to work out the percentage of how much of a book I'd read, and the pleasure at knowing such a thing was a powerful boost to my self-esteem. It excited me. Sometimes it scared me to think that if I'd not met the right people when I did, my educational interest may have withered like a neglected plant.

There was no way my captain was going to let this version fail because I, as the captain, gave strict orders to nurture this version seriously.

One of the teachers said to me something that would change my direction once again. I had a good relationship with her and mentioned that one day I'd like to write. She replied that she could see me in print one day, and that I should go to university. The seed was planted, the roots grew thick and strong, and soon enough the fruit was known. To not be deterred by a poor start and push on regardless is something I admire in others and often it is the decision to act on a thought which is the hardest part of any plan.

My plan was to pass the exam I had failed the previous year. I had almost nothing but thoughts of university in my mind. I began to apply for places. I didn't quite know how I got to it, but I decided on a joint degree of philosophy and Spanish. I started to have interviews, and at one prestigious university, I had a meeting with a professor. On a board behind his desk was a syllogism. I immediately recognised it, having read about them in my copy of *A History of Western Philosophy*. After a while he asked me about it. I explained it to him. He said that's about as hard as it gets. In the end I chose a different university as they offered the joint degree that I wanted. I later passed the exam and for the first time in my life I had earned a certificate that did not have brickwork or swimming written on it. A usual degree lasts three years, but because I was doing a language, I had an extra year at a university in Spain or some other country that spoke Spanish. My next four years were planned. My plans for life were getting longer and more specific. I phoned a builder to see if he had work for the months before I started university. He said he had too much. Now I could save money to back up my grant.

I used to trudge to building sites feeling downtrodden. I remember praying to a god (any god) to change me into a man so I could take charge of my life; yet it never dawned on me that God expected me to do it myself.

But no learning or changing for the better can assuage the onset of mental health issues that caused me debilitating mind pain. It came like tides I could not deter, surging over my deck, and it was all I could do to stop my crew from abandoning ship.

Looking back from my present vantage point, I see first the anger, where almost anything or anyone could get me snarling. Then I began to take risks and let go of the tiller, but the worst of all was the feeling that comes which I can only describe as a brooding, sinister hatred of everything *out there*. I sensed a presence pervading *my space*. It came less when I got to know it better and learned some management techniques, but for early versions, well they just sought alcohol and drugs and waited for it to pass. Early versions felt a crippling weight bearing down on their immature minds. Not one of us ever took a prescribed drug that helped. The only substances that did help were alcohol and marijuana. They worked because they immediately changed the feeling and the mood, but at the same time I was wiring my brain to rely on them. Although I felt immediate relief, people I lived with or worked with bore the brunt of me *getting better.*

That's how my first marriage failed. That's how I lost valuable friends. And that's how I could never hold down a job for any reasonable amount of time. I just reconciled that this was a part of my makeup, a flaw in my personality, and assumed my life would always be that way. I believed I'd remain alone because I couldn't put anyone through mind pain times again. Some of those *low* periods lasted three months or more. I had high peaks followed by low troughs. Going from living in great places with good friends, money and work, to almost seamlessly waking up in a miserable place with no hope or options, passing from one situation to another like sitting on a lump of driftwood as it meandered from here to there, guided by nothing other than the vagaries of tide and weather. Once I started to count how many places I'd lived. When I reached a ridiculous amount so swiftly, I gave up as the true number must be obscene.

Outside help can be useful, but inner desire is essential. Not all advice is valuable; some of it is beyond contempt.

I remember that pre-university version in a bedsit in southeast London. He was one of the happiest versions because although he had building site work lined up, the money saved would go to keeping him studying at university for four years. And yet, without any warning, one of the worst bouts of mind pain hit him at the very moment he was contemplating a life improved. *He* was reading a popular self-development book, which stated that depressed people often like to remain in that state because they like the secondary gain, as the author calls it, of attention from people.

That writer can never have experienced true depression. He must have been mistaking the words, thinking of people who think low thoughts, get worried and became miserable or mope around, because I can assure him that when it comes to mind pain, it is not a feeling of being down, it is a feeling of mental pain that hurts as physical pain hurts.

When struck by mind pain, I have never wanted attention, only to be alone, which is one of the causes, along with others, why I could never hold down a relationship or a job. It is also why almost every version always turned to alcohol and illegal drugs for relief. And this is how addictions are caused because everyone is looking to change their feeling from pain to relief, or at least from pain to less pain.

But that pre-university version kept going, and although demons often snatched the helm away from me, I as the captain wrestled it back long enough to bear the pain, to keep working – saving money for the coming of university. And I remember the day that that version handed over the reins to the next one.

He wrote in a journal, "I have managed to carry on and earn the money so that you might study in relative peace, and when mind pain comes, you will be able to rest and tell them you are just unwell. I am hoping that I and other versions who have worked on site was enough to enable you to remain free from that. I wish you well in your studies".

And with that, a mental bridge formed and over it the next one crossed.

Gary Troia

Chapter 19

A man sooner or later discovers that he is the master-gardener of his soul, the director of his life.

James Allen

Feelings of low self-esteem began to surface as university drew near. The only university graduates I'd ever known were Fiona and her friends. I was reminded by negative thinking how I failed the A Level English Literature Certificate, and university was not going to be for me, and I would fail miserably. These were recurring thoughts that I had to deal with and dismiss daily.

Five minutes' walk up the road from where I lived was a small independent bookshop, which was well stocked with philosophy. I spent more on books each week than I did on drink and drugs. I didn't really go out anymore. I got to know the woman whose shop it was. She started to give me advice about what to read. After a time, I started to take tea and cake with her in the afternoons, debating all manner of subjects. Across the road I watched builders working on scaffolding. I kept thinking that it could easily be me over there listening to never-ending football talk instead of philosophy in a bookshop. I saw this as a personal education, like a gift from the gods. If I ever had mind pain, I would not go, as our relationship was a rare and fragile gift, and I didn't want to break it by an unwanted outbreak or outburst.

My relationship with the bookstore owner stood me in good stead, strengthening my confidence and pacifying problematic thoughts. The week before university, I started to read Homer's *Odyssey*. I don't know why, but I felt it necessary. It wasn't. On the train on that first morning, my feelings were a mixture of hope, excitement and nagging concern that I might be out of my depth. It was a long journey from southeast London to north London, thinking thoughts of negative - positive, like a long tennis rally.

I thought about four years of study ahead - a four-year plan. I was not going to get side-tracked by anything. I put Homer down and maybe for the first time ever, thought deeply about discipline, because above all it was discipline that would see me through.

I was expecting to meet the odd Plato strolling around. I didn't. I realised I wasn't a genius, but I also realised that I was not out of my depth. I made some new acquaintances. I debated subjects that I had always been interested in but never knew much about. Soon enough my level of education caught up. I thought of Fiona and her friends, and how they now seemed like ordinary people. There was no going back to any old ways, places, relationships or thinking. That was too dangerous. It is an often-used military tactic of burning your bridges (or ships) so there is no escape, and that you either fight hard or die. I was going to fight to remain on the other side of the bridge I'd worked so hard to cross.

The biggest trouble I had was getting my Spanish to a decent level. I spent hours in the language department trying to understand current Spanish news with earphones on. At first, I thought it was going to be impossible, as the harder I tried the harder it became. The day I thought, well, I'm never going to understand and relaxed, was the day the newsreaders' voices spoke to me.

My first exam was philosophy. Two friends and I took cocaine in the toilet cubicles. I sat looking at my paper, ravenous to start. I felt like a crazy madman. I wrote like I'd just received the gift of exam wizardry. The only trouble was that watery snot dripped from my nose onto the paper, making some of the words illegible after I wiped it away.

The hardest exam of all was a philosophy exam in Spanish. As we were waiting for the signal to start, I noticed our lecturer walk in and sit at the front. She was there for moral support, as she knew how hard it was. But instead of helping, her presence signified how hard it was going to be and concerned me more than before sighting her. I turned the paper and saw words that may have been in any language that I'd never heard of, for all it mattered. I couldn't understand the question. My mind was as dense as a concrete block. Eventually I worked out some of the linking words, but the important ones I couldn't. I kept trying to work the question out on paper and wished I had taken cocaine again. I looked up at the clock and thirty-five minutes had passed. I scanned the room and everyone else was writing. I put my pen down and closed my eyes. I'd come far, and to be fair, I was doing a philosophy exam in a foreign language when only four years ago I had failed an English language exam. I'd begun a Spanish course at university with no previous Spanish lessons, sat in classes with bi-lingual speakers, so there was nothing to be ashamed about; maybe I'd just gone too far too soon.

After some minutes of contemplating, a sense of peace enveloped me like a warming cup of cocoa on a winter's evening. It looked as though I'd fallen at the last fence, but it was a big fence and a difficult course. I settled down within my space and congratulated myself on coming so far. I was content and relaxed. I decided that I was going to get up soon and walk away from the paper. But as that thought left me, I sensed something come to the fore and noticed that it was looking at the question. It urged me to pick up my pen and start to write what seemed to be dictated to me. Spanish words bubbled up from a teaming river within me then flowed out onto the page. And I knew instinctively that all I had to do was stay out of the way. Before I knew it the paper was finished. I looked at what had been written.

My lecturer, from Colombia, could not stop talking about me passing the exam to anyone that would listen. I didn't let my ego dine out on it because I knew *I* had little or nothing to do with it. A Spanish University is next...

I Return to Versions of Myself

Gary Troia

Chapter 20

Oh, how I hated discipline, and my heart despised reproof!
Proverbs 5:12

I'm at the airport earlier than necessary because it's time to evaluate. Airports for me are either good or bad and nothing in between. Most people see airports as no more than a transport hub; but for me they are mostly a beginning or an end of something more significant than a mere holiday. Leaving was generally better than returning, but there were exceptions.

Before change, a version could *be*, as one version coined it: *in liquid neutrality,* which meant that *I* should wait for instruction before transfiguration to another version. Walking round the airport's shops and bars without thinking ahead or behind. It's the closest I ever got to feeling like the Buddha felt in a glorious present moment. In many ways it was the best meditation I could ever muster because being in the airport was like a kind of insulation from the past that lurked outside the airport doors, and the future was at the end of a flight that had yet to begin. Anything was possible as there are so many destinations and so many versions.

There were routines to follow, though. The right bottle from the scent shop had to be well considered before spraying myself to match the mood of the journey ahead.

Soon my sauntering would come to an end, as it was time for a drink and a think on a seat by a window that enabled me to view the planes that came and went.

At first, I thought of nothing, but soon thoughts and comparisons began to push by fragile mental barriers.

I made the comparison with the flight to the U.S. I didn't know what lay ahead of me then and how much time I would spend there, but this time I know where I'm going and have a year of academic study.

Once I'm belted in, time begins. Liquid neutrality begins to take shape into a new version. The descent into Spain got me thinking: How green and hilly – almost like Switzerland.

I used my Spanish for the first time when I gave the taxi driver directions.

The room in the halls of residence was like a pleasant prison cell. There was a bed, a small wooden table, a wooden chair and a thin rectangular window where I stood and stared at the city below. I wondered what would happen. Who would I meet? I arrived one month before university began to get acclimatised. I stayed looking out over the city for some time. I thought back to the version sitting on the bench at Heathrow Airport, lost and alone, drained of hope. I thought about hopelessness. *I* had almost lost all hope then.

The view of the city, although so foreign, seemed comforting. I felt a presence as if a wise watcher stood with me nodding to that feeling. It made me smile.

The halls of residence were up such a steep road that it took great care walking down, and a huge effort walking up. Every morning I strolled down the hill and spent most of the day wandering. Other versions had spent many days on package holidays in the south of Spain, but the north was different. There were no British bars, nowhere you could get an English breakfast, and that was good. There were no English signs, and no one seemed to speak English.

Whenever I needed to buy something, I rehearsed the words in my mind. I tried to avoid, as much as possible, loud or busy places.

Often when I asked for something, I was unable to understand the reply, as they spoke too fast, and the accent was difficult to decipher. In the city I spent hours sitting at bars, watching nothing and everything.

I thought of nothing for much of the time, nothing about the past, nothing about the future. I was a foreigner in a foreign land, and it was the best position I could think of being in. If someone spoke and I did not want to talk, I just said: *Lo siento, no hablo Español.* That gave me an idea for when I returned to

England – if I did not want to talk, I could just say: *Lo siento, no hablo Ingles.*

One day I got a hankering for a full English breakfast, so I decided to walk back from the city to where I lived to find a bar, as it was quieter. I chose one and ordered the usual ingredients of an English breakfast. Soon a plate of tomatoes was delivered to my table. Next came a plate of mushrooms, then a plate of ham followed. One of two things was happening: I must have ordered badly, or they were taking the piss. The eggs came next. I did not worry what was happening because I decided to eat it all.

There was a bar that I favoured. It was always either empty or busy, and nothing in between. I began to nod and have small chats with the owner. I would have a book to read or sometimes I studied Spanish grammar or read children's books in Spanish. The owner would laugh when he brought my drink and saw what I was reading. But apart from that I kept on with no real thinking, although random thoughts did start to emerge. "This is good. No one knows you here; you can be who you want to be". I then got what Jesus had said about *a prophet having no honour in his own country*. I don't consider the word prophet here as applying to me, but I do consider it correct when meaning that no one is allowed to completely change from what they once were and be accepted as that change in the place they grew up. "Oh", they say, "it's just him going through a phase". And therefore, you must leave or forever be labelled as that which you are now not.

I saw that no matter how much a person changed, no one from my past would ever allow me to renew and transform. People from the past, when you meet them, have a crystalised version of you, indeed anyone that meets you again judges you from an image they have made for you. And if you remain changed it reveals a distance between you, which causes them to be jealous or angry. They would rather you repeat your mistakes that keep you in the past instead of making changes, as it makes them feel better at not having changed themselves

I started to feel myself expand into a greater space. A flood of thoughts poured into my mind.

I remember telling certain people before I left, including family members, that I was thinking of becoming a teacher. Each of their responses was a combination of laughter, disbelief and amusement. The version that listened to those responses did the right thing by cutting them off. I began to think about who I wanted to be in the future, far away from their petty ridicule.

I had come along way. I had education and was close to being bi-lingual. I was studying at one of the best universities in Spain, and I was miles away from laying bricks. I looked around at the people in the bar and it came to my attention that most of the people I was looking at dressed much better than the majority in Britain – at least smarter.

I began to visualise myself in different sets of clothes. I had always bucked fashion trends and had my own style, so I had a good start. I had saved a fair amount of money, so I got up and headed into the centre of the city to see what I could find.

I returned with clothes different to what I usually

wore in England, enough to identify an outwardly different version of myself when I looked in the mirror. I looked through the window overlooking the city, and for the first time in my life envisioned a future version that would be the best version; I was going to grow into something that was once unrealistic and incomprehensible to old versions.

For the first time, I began to create a version in my mind that had higher values and more integrity. I would keep acting out my new self until it became habit, until one day, I would walk into that version and live and be *him* in the manner envisioned.

With caution I thought back to fallow times in a bedsit, drinking and taking drugs to ward off the fear of going to a building site in the morning, or to ease mind pain. Now I was somewhere else, walking around with confidence. I thought of my doubters. I thought of my father's phrases that "I wasn't worth a light" and "a waste of space". I never felt pride, just a sense of achievement and satisfaction, and the wisdom that I could become almost anything, like anyone can, if they reach within and search for their authenticity.

Days later, sitting in my local bar, the bar owner beckoned me over and introduced me to a Spanish woman because she could speak English. We had a chat. Then she left for work. About half an hour later the phone rang. The owner picked it up and made the gesture with the phone that it was for me. It was the woman. She asked if I wanted to go out that evening.

Two weeks later I no longer walked up and down the steep hill of the halls of residence because I had moved in with the woman from the bar. She had an amazing penthouse apartment. She worked for her father who was a local entrepreneur. In a few short weeks, I had gone from looking through the narrow rectangle window of a soulless cell with plastic cutlery, to standing on a large balcony in a fine apartment in an expensive part of town. I barely knew anyone at university because I had a ready-made set of friends that she knew.

Although the changes I made were lasting, still mind pain came from time to time. I still had no real understanding of it. I forgot that I had to take time, see these episodes out, and look after myself while the storm in my head passed. But instead, I tried to battle on through, fight the problem, but this course of action only exacerbated things.

This relationship was long, lasting an academic year. We stayed together throughout it, but the connection had sagged between us. I learnt so much from her and my year in that city, that it became an integral part of me. As the plane took off for London, I once again thought what I was flying into next. Through the window I watched the city that I had been a part of, lived a life in, recede, and then vanish from view.

I Return to Versions of Myself

Gary Troia

Chapter 21

*The two most important days in your life are the day you are
born and the day you find out why.*

Mark Twain

The last year at university was the worst one because
it was a countdown to the end of a plan, and I didn't
have another one for what comes next.

I recall looking back to when I was on the train on
the first day, thinking I had a four-year plan, and
thought how long that was, but how naïve to miss
thinking about what I was going to do at the end of
those four years. I suppose it was the longest plan I
had ever had and therefore it seemed to that version
close enough to forever. There were no major
problems, just that I missed the previous year in Spain
and was concerned at the ending of the academic
year. It was helpful, however, knowing that I was
progressing in other areas.

In that final year I tried to put a break on time. A total of five years (including the one at college) of studying were finishing. Five years of following a path were running out. I started to feel anxious that I was heading back to building sites.

I applied for many jobs. Almost never got an answer. I supposed it might have had something to do with intermittent building work and time spent with no explanation of what I did in between that wasn't going to get me far. I thought my ploy of transparency and honesty would somehow work in my favour. This is where naivety let me down again. I had to believe that I would not go back, but I was in constant civil war with the opposite belief. I started longing for the previous year in Spain. My lifestyle had dropped. I was sharing a flat. I remembered the words of Fiona: "Philosophy and Spanish? Really? Why aren't you studying something that'll earn you a decent living"?

I saw her point, but I chose what I enjoyed. Was that also a naïve decision that might put my future in jeopardy? I came late to the world of structure and commitment. I still thought about writing, feeling sometimes I could do it and at other times not. I chose philosophy for learning to write precisely, and Spanish for understanding how language worked and was formed.

Then, like a coin dropped into an empty piggy bank came a thought into my mind. Before starting university, I had told family and acquaintances that I was going to become a teacher. I'd forgotten all about it. I remembered their laughter, so that was what I decided to do. In many ways it was an outlandish idea for me, but it did plant a seed.

Teaching was not a dream; only something to achieve and accomplish that was way out of my usual. I created a vision of myself teaching. At first, I found it amusing just like family members and acquaintances did. I remembered how I'd left school with no qualifications, having never read a book, and was semi-illiterate. Whereas many other school leavers had left with qualifications and a plan, while that version left with a massive appetite for rebellion and self-destruction and achieved both and more besides. The only thing that stood in my way were my poor beliefs from a programmed past.

I Return to Versions of Myself

Gary Troia

Chapter 22

"…people who pity themselves go on pitying themselves even when they are laid softly on a cushion…"

Dale Carnegie

I saw myself on a conveyor belt that was coming to a drop off point, and I was about to fall off it into a building site. Five years of study only to find myself back where I started. Except I wasn't back where I started because now I knew about a different life, and those memories were likely to add to my angst and make it worse than ever when I was in a trench or high up on a scaffold in winter.

Money was also running out. I cut back as much as I could and tried to delay the inevitable. I willed something to arrive over the hill, but I knew innately that was not how it worked, I had to allow opportunities to take their course. I vowed to let go of the past and let the future work itself out.

The times when things go well is when I am in alignment with myself and have no regrets or random hopes and wishes of what I want to happen next, but the more I tried to force authenticity, the further it moved out of reach. So, I began to concentrate on every little thing I did. If I washed dishes, I focused on the water falling from the tap with wonder. Focusing on water is recognition of being alive. I homed in on objects I saw when walking, wondering whether I knew them at all, and it worked in keeping my predicament at bay. I concluded I was good at swimming, because it was meditative. Once I found a rhythm, I just kept going, one arm after the other, legs pounding a rhythmical beat.

I walked through a park each day to a local shop and bought *The London Evening Standard*. Those in the building trades bought it when looking for a job. You could tell if the economy was doing well by counting the building jobs available and you could take your pick, but when it swung in the opposite direction, it was tough, there was hardly any work and those that were working stayed where they were, no matter the wage being paid.

The paper advertised many other jobs. I tried to ignore the building section and looked for something else – anything else. The only jobs I'd ever done other than bricklaying, were delivering drugs, landscape gardening, and cleaning chandeliers in central London.

But there was nothing there I thought I could do. I went for interviews for tele sales, but all of them were commission only and I couldn't be sure if I would earn enough to keep me going.

Without my permission, something within me turned to the construction section. I looked down the list, my focus hooked on one of the bricklaying jobs that was not worded like the others: "Bricklaying tutor required". I sat down on a bench in the park and reread it. I had never thought about teaching brickwork. I supposed I hadn't because I wanted to get as far away from building as possible.

But there it was, a job that was linked to bricklaying, yet teaching. I could go to work in one place and not have to travel from one site to the next. I went home and applied. Was this what I was waiting for? Was this an opportunity coming down the hill, or was it a mirage? I expected a reply within a couple of weeks. I began to think that maybe it was a mirage. By now my time was up and I was working on a site that was walking distance from my shared flat. It was winter – a cold winter. Before we started work, we had to take off the hessian that covered the brickwork, but still there were parts that weren't covered properly so we had to smash the ice from the frogs of the bricks. I was beginning to lose faith in myself and felt the vibration of my life degrade to a level I hadn't felt for years. Angry entities lead the way, and I became loose and uncaring, like sitting astride driftwood again and letting the devil push me around like a toy. I remember looking up at the sky, looking desperately for something to blame; the sky was looming with filthy dark clouds in the distance, heavily pregnant with rain, and all of it was coming my way.

I knew that this batch of bad weather was going to stop work. I was always happy when bad weather struck, and we had to go home. Money was always secondary. Even my anger had died down because I was at such a low ebb, and now I just needed to be at home and self-isolate with drink and drugs. As I walked the ten minutes back to the flat, I calculated that I had enough money to just be and not bother about work, for a while. I needed to be alone and let my inner storm play out. There was nothing else to do. In some ways working as a self-employed bricklayer had one benefit, you could just walk off a site and never go back, and no one really cared, as there was always someone to replace you.

Another good part was that my roommate had gone back to the north of England for the Christmas holidays, and I would be alone and not have to converse with anyone. There have been many times in the lives of versions when mind pain came down like talons of a large bird of prey, gripping *my* mind ever tighter. Being alone, however, was a magnificent feeling, almost an antidote to mind pain. I could go to bed when I wanted, eat when I wanted, and think of nothing at all. It was like my own personal retreat from the dramas *out there*.

One morning there was a knock at the door. Usually when I recuperate the door is never answered, but that day I opened it. The postman handed me a parcel. This was an unexpected occurrence. I took it upstairs. I lit a joint. I ripped off the wrapping to reveal a book. It was a biography of Charles Bukowski from a friend of mine at university.

I read the blurb on the back and got interested. I began to read and by late evening I'd finished it. The book got me thinking differently, something that most books do not. I had always entertained the idea of writing, but there was always a voice that mocked me, saying, "Just because you have completed a degree after years of having no clue, does not give you the right to think you now do have a clue and can write".

But here was someone writing about being a drunk and living with whores and doing menial work just to get by to drink and write again. Even though I'd been to university, I was still naïve about what existed in the world of literature, and the demons and mental health issues that I have carried from a child made me doubt myself, although less so than before.

I will always be grateful to my friend for that gift, because it changed my thinking again, all new changes in thinking are an expansion of the mind, and once stretched, it can never return to its previous dimensions.

I was so full of energy and ideas having read the biography that I was eager to read Bukowski's novels, but it was Christmas Eve. I went and put together a festive meal of cold meats and cheese from Marks and Spencer's and decided to go into central London after boxing day to get *Post Office* and anything else they had by Bukowski. The wait seemed like a prison sentence. I soon bought two of his novels and read them in a day.

The following day I was pacing about. I tried to listen to my voice of reason, tried to follow its advice. Sometimes I found it hard to believe in it when my demons started squawking and chirping, urging me to get up to no good and find pleasure in that. But I persevered and spent my days walking long distances to tire myself out.

I thought nothing about money or what I would have to do when it ran out. I thought nothing about the past and couldn't care less about the future. Occasionally I smiled at the knowledge that my lack of attention was aggravating certain entities within. One day I returned to the flat to find an assortment of mail. Some rubbish, some brown envelopes, but there was something different, it was a letter with a business heading, the heading of the training centre where I had applied for a position. I had forgotten all about it. Inside the envelope was an offer of an interview.

I can see that version now, walking a bridge over the Thames on a windy day for an interview. A strong gust of wind whips the scarf off his neck. A voice at the time said, "Look, your bad luck is returning, you are not destined for this". But he smiles, lets it pass, and watches his red tartan scarf on the water, like an eel, snaking its way down the Thames.

When things are right, they are right. The two men that interviewed me were ex bricklayers and I immediately got on with them. I left thinking how well and easy it had gone. Having a degree as well as bricklaying experience and certificates had set me apart.

I decided to take the train to Central London to look for new reading material. As I walked out of the station at Charing Cross, I received a call. It was an unknown number. I didn't usually answer unknowns, but I was feeling good and answered it. It was the training centre. They offered me the job.

It dawned on him that he was off building sites. I am a teacher, he told himself. He wanted to ring those who had laughed at him. But soon listened to a voice that told him it was undignified. The trouble was that there was no one to tell about his good news. He scanned his phone and the only name he found who he thought might be pleased was the Jamaican woman that lived next door to his gran. She was truly pleased. Then off he sauntered in search of something new to read.

Gary Troia

Chapter 23

*If you really want to escape the things that harass you, what
you're needing is not to be in a different place but to be a
different person.*

Seneca

The night before starting work as a teacher was a
strange one. If I knew how a butterfly felt on the
point of metamorphosis, I might call it that. On a
table on the other side of the room were my clothes
for the following day. They were clean and what I
would choose to wear casually. However, this was a
crossover period as I still needed my old boots and
jeans for the days in the workshop – I hadn't escaped
bricklaying entirely, but I had escaped building sites.

All my life I'd tried to escape, and this is the moment
I climbed over the wall. I looked back and covered
my route over time and the pain that went with it. I
had no nerves at all – in fact, I was less anxious than
if I were going to a building site on the first day. I was

more than qualified, although I lacked the joy of a subject that good teachers need.

I walked to the station with my bag full of pens instead of a bag full of tools. I viewed the other passengers and especially builders going to site. I didn't feel pride like I thought I might, but a sense of deep relief. I had achieved what I'd set out to do, so it was a matter of closing my eyes and taking deep breaths of relief. Although this was a long-held idea, I'd always been unsure as to whether it would come true, often I thought I was fated or cursed to never leave sites.

When I got going, I naturally preferred classroom work because it reminded me of studying in colleges and universities as opposed to the practical work which was close enough to a real building site, except that the mortar had lime rather than cement so the walls could be knocked down and the mortar reused.

I did a deal with the other brickwork tutor to take his class for theory work as he preferred the built environment, and I was more than happy to let him take my group for practical.

Yet because of the type of training centre - the people they enrolled had some serious mental problems - I began to lose sight of my own. I was more like a counsellor than a brickwork tutor. What with that and not addressing my own mental health, I suddenly took a turn for the worse and had no other option than to self-isolate. I had been working at the centre for over two years.

I had holiday pay for the first time in my life, but I didn't enjoy it as much as the versions that had money and isolated from building sites, as I knew there were many students that were relying on me. I became guilty, which didn't help my self-isolation. I thought of the man I was teaching who had lost his job in the textile business and was retraining to support his family. There were many others like him alongside some very problematic people who seemed to me that they were in the wrong place, but the training centre would take anyone for the sake of money. This group that I had nurtured, never left my mind, so I vowed to go back after a week and see them through their final part of their course. It was hard work, and I was being overrun by chaotic demons. I was falling out with members of staff. But I saw the group through. In a meeting I looked around the place and knew I had to leave for my own health. At lunch I went outside and rang a subcontractor I often worked with and did the unthinkable, I asked if he had any work. He did, and that day I went and gave my notice. The managers tried to persuade me to rethink but I had to get out. I felt I was in an open jail rather than doing hard time, but it was a jail, nevertheless. From overseeing the students, I spent the rest of the day like someone who had no idea how to interact with anyone. I had to be home and home alone. I opened wine, smoked a joint and let all sorts of crazy thought trains through my station. I had no idea what I had done or what I was about to do. It seemed like I had regressed into a poorer version from the past.

But soon enough the realisation that I didn't have to go back to that job outweighed any concern of life back in the wild building sites. I never knew that I was literally convalescing at the time; I just couldn't do anything else anyway. Later versions acquired this knowledge about convalescing and so were better prepared for it.

I took control of my thoughts and dismissed any negative ones that came. Now I was aware and reasonably in charge. Yet almost all the traffic was negative, and it was tiring to deal with so much of it.

When my student called and thanked me for helping him gain his certificate, I told him that I had called a sub-contractor and had got him a job. His joy was palpable. A week later he told me that he was working for him and doing well. He then invited me round his house for curry and a drink. That night I was received with the upmost respect from him, his wife and daughters. I don't think I've ever felt so truly humbled in all my life. It was what I needed to hear, that I had helped to change someone's life for the better, and that was enough to get me thinking how much better one feels when focused on someone else's needs rather than your own incessant yapping ego.

Gary Troia

Chapter 24

I will not think that I know what must remain beyond my

present grasp.

A course in miracles

As the turbulence of having resigned began to dissipate, I received a call from a sub-contractor who said he would like to come and see me. And although I knew him well, his request was highly irregular.

He arrived Saturday morning and drove me to a house that needed work. The drive was longer than I expected. We left the London suburbs and entered the countryside. Finally, we turned down a driveway that was long and came to a lovely detached house with a small lake. Part of the house needed pointing. Two thirds were already completed. The owners were away for two months, and my job was to finish it and stay in a flat connected to the house. I agreed and moved in two days later. Pointing is nothing like bricklaying. It is often renovation work. It's quiet and requires a deft touch. It was like being offered a retreat from madness.

He dropped me off with my supplies. I unloaded crates of wine, a large bag of grass, and some food and water. Everything in its perfect order. While he was explaining the job and the time limit I had to do it, I just wanted him to leave. Soon enough I watched his van diminish in size to that of a toy car. I laughed. I felt my joy rising in proportion to the distance growing between us. I was on the verge of excitement as I saw glimpses of his white van through the row of birch trees lining the road that was taking him away.

A new awareness arose, which brought on a huge sense of relief. Like a wet dog I shook off my cares and worries. I had been granted a space to be alone in an area where I knew no one, and at the same time had work that was accommodating to my sense of mind. I went about changing my thoughts, visualising, making plans, and becoming more disciplined. It was like taking safe harbour for a while. I soon felt health begin to surge and rise throughout my body, mind, and soul.

I entered the flat and acquainted myself with it. It was smart and comfortable. It seemed neither alien nor unwelcoming. A smile stretched wide. I tried to think of the last time I felt so free but gave up because it didn't matter. I kept inhaling long deep breaths of country air and appreciated the relative silence. In the bedroom I took out my clothes from my suitcase and neatly placed them in the wardrobe and drawers. Unpacked some books and piled them against a wall under a window that looked out on a large garden and the small lake. I rolled a joint and went to discover the gardens and make myself known to them.

I felt at ease sitting on a tree stump, watching ducks on the lake go about their way. The light of a spring sun turned the water a magical golden hue. For some reason unknown to me, I blessed the garden and lake, then went and looked at the job that laid in wait. There was a lot of pointing to be done, and it had to be weather pointed, which takes a little time and skill to get right, as the angle of the bed joints and perp joints must neither be too flat nor too acute. I looked at what had been done and memorised the style in order to replicate it. The scaffold was already in place, so all I had to do was knock up a gauge of mortar, take a bucket to where I was going to work, and get it done.

The peace within me was a deep spiritual peace that I rarely felt. I was so alone in that place but so connected with everything. I felt a strange and deep love for the house and the surrounding gardens and lake, and somehow knew it was reciprocated. The spliff was strong but not enough to make a wonderful mindset happen alone, because as the days went by, it not only remained with me, but increased.

When my day's work was done, I carried a book to a bench by the lake and alternated between reading or staring into the lake. I was rereading *The Brothers' Karamazov* and dipping in and out of James Allen's *As a Man Thinketh*.

In a shed by the side of the house were some antiquated carpentry tools and an old bike with a basket on front. I began riding up and down the driveway. About three miles away was a grocery store

in a village. I used to walk there and back for
provisions. One day I took two wheels – I could not
stop laughing as I rode the bike with a basket on the
front. I had the feeling that I was in England in the
fifties, living a simple life. The only persons I ever
spoke with while at the house were the woman in the
grocery store, the odd person or farmer on the way to
the shop and back, and the postman.

The job went well and quicker than I'd envisioned. I
slowed down a little because I did not want my
tranquil haven to end. This was one of the most self-
contained and happy versions of myself that ever was.
I worried about nothing and was grateful for
everything. But as *we* know, all good things come to
an end. The last page of this chapter was turned as I
waited outside on the drive. I saw a flash of white van
through the trees before it turned into the drive,
coming to take me away and plonk me back into the
river of life. I accepted it and put my faith into
believing that it was going to be well if I just let it be.
I had taken refuge in a harbour for a few weeks, and
now I was sailing back into deep tidal waters but with

an unchartered course.

There were two major realisations at that time: "I am not all bad", which sounded strange when I'd said it out loud, for being bad had been entrenched in early versions from a father that used to say often: "You're not worth a light". When I said it to myself, I just couldn't stop smiling. I no longer had the need to be right or prove naysayers wrong that I could do what I set out to do. I considered that it was necessary to rid myself of such people and find like-minded others who I wanted to be around, people that changed their lives for the better. It was all so simple.

I also understood that you must never tell anyone of your plans. The old saying, *a trouble shared is a trouble halved* is true because it loses its strength when you share it, but if you tell someone your plans, it has the same effect, but in the sense of weakening them, which is not what you want to do.

With my newfound way forward, I was about to sail on, but this time with discipline, forward thinking, and a plan to get where I wanted to be, wherever that was. I had a fine ship instead of a lump of driftwood. I had enough money to stay in harbour and work out where my destination would be, and I used the time to visualise what kind of captain I should become.

It dawned on me that visualisation was not something new, I had always been doing it, because it was my visualisation that created the situations or opportunities that emerged on the hill. What was going to be different this time was that I would have discipline and readiness to accept them and enhance them, rather than just react and let the opportunities slip from my grasp. In a way it was like when I used to pray for something, get it, but not being able to use it properly because I was never prepared enough to nurture what I received.

I recalled a friend of mine in the training centre who had moved on to a college to work. At the time I paid little attention because I thought that it was too similar. He told me about the TES (*Times Educational Supplement*). Again, I was slow on the uptake. I realised that this was a proper career in education in colleges rather than a training centre. I started to buy the *TES* and couldn't believe how many jobs were available.

Within the first paper I bought, there were opportunities all over the country. A whole new world had opened. No longer *The London Evening Standard*. Just this thought alone elevated and expanded my horizon.

Soon came letters in the post from colleges. One was in the north of England, and I went and stayed for a week. The next was a college close to where I was brought up. Because I was blasé about getting that job, I got that job.

I Return to Versions of Myself

Gary Troia

Chapter 25

Vision is the act of seeing what is invisible to others.
Jonathan Swift

I took the job. This was a strange homecoming. I had travelled far in search of a job away from building sites, and the first professional job away from them was back where I started out. The night before, I replayed the memories of going to school and the stages after and couldn't quite grasp the fact that I was about to become a lecturer, but more to the point was how anyone would allow me to be a lecturer; so the dark nagging voice started. It was interesting to see which thinking would take the lead. I had belief in myself, but my history of mind pain, and occasional low self-esteem confronted me often in the battle of being worthy to teach a new generation.

The demon of low self-esteem was chirping in my ear. But I counteracted those thoughts with the knowledge that I had proved so many people who had laughed at the idea that I could possibly teach, wrong. They stood in stark contrast to those that did believe in me and urged me on, none of which were old friends or family. If you have a dream of any kind, and if anyone laughs at it, they are the ones to stay away from. Not only will you do yourself a huge favour, but life also becomes easier and more joyful without them. Once you have an idea of what you want to do, create a vision until it feels normal, and then formulate and follow a plan, and soon you will find yourself living that situation you envisioned. Soon being a lecturer felt the same as being a bricklayer.

The trouble with colleges and vocational teaching is that you have no idea how to teach, and you are just thrust into it, as opposed to schoolteachers who must go through a teaching qualification first.

I never expected to show up and be told that I was going to take a class at 9.am. I assumed someone would go through the curriculum with me - maybe shadow a class or at least be formerly introduced to it. The manager of the department, I soon found out, was interested in little but doing little.

I insisted that I shadow him, as I didn't know what to teach, so reluctantly the manager took the class. What he proceeded to do was get them to read from a book in turns, it was like watching teaching from a Victorian time.

I scanned the room and saw how bored they were. I was bored. At break time I was so irritated at what I'd witnessed that I said I would take over. It only took minutes of getting to know the group by talking to them authentically that the atmosphere completely changed.

It went well. I moved from the other side of London and got a flat. I made good friendships with some of the other lecturers, even going on holiday with one of them. Then one night, after about a year, a bout of mind pain arrived, the like of which I'd not experienced for so long. I was writhing in my bed all night like a heroin addict going cold turkey, sweat pouring from my head and I didn't know what to do or where to go. Sometimes drinking solved the problem briefly, but even spirits, which I never usually drank, could not match up to this heavyweight bout of mind pain.

I couldn't stay still. And the torture never stopped. Going from one room to another, having a bath and minutes later having a shower. I thought about the parable of Jesus driving the legion of demons from the mad man and allowing them to go into a herd of pigs before hurtling off a cliff. What I wouldn't have given for Jesus to do the same for me that night.

The excruciating pain was still there in the morning. It is difficult to call work and say you are sick with mind pain, as that will be the end of your reputation. The principal had come up to me and said she had heard good things about me. And now she was about to hear bad things about me. It is far easier to talk about mental health than it ever used to be, but it will take generations for it to be excepted and treated like any other human ailment. Most of the time I just need a break from dealing with outside issues.

I was in such a state that I violently snapped at a

manager. I shouldn't have gone in. Another manager sent me home. Back at home I knew it was all over.

When I came to my senses, everything I had worked for was gone, vanished into nothing once again. I felt back on driftwood, surely on my way to building sites, still trying to make sense of why and how the mind pain comes. Replacing a white board marker for a trowel again.

It is hard when the mental illness leaves, because you now must deal with the guilt, shame, regret, and the aftermath and consequences of it. You know how far it is to get back. It is clear what has happened, but it is not clear how long it will take to repair your battered ship and sail again. I had recovered time after time, but how long before there is no desire left, before the ship is wrecked beyond repair or even sunk?

Gary Troia

Chapter 26

Our globe seemed all too small for the youthful Alexander:
unhappily he chafed at this world's narrow confines, as though
caged on some bare rocky Aegean islet. Yet when he entered the
city of brick-walled Babylon, a coffin was to suffice him.

Juvenal

I yearned to get away and be alone, but I needed
money, so I found building work and put all I had
into it, as if I wanted to be the most professional
tradesman on site. The reason was to forget all
negative thinking about sites and earn as much as I
could before flying away, but this also had the effect
of bringing me to the attention of the owner, who
started giving me better jobs and more responsibility.
I diversified and almost enjoyed work.

After time my mind slowed down as I had removed
myself from situational dilemmas and dramas acting
out in the world, which I would normally react to. I
began to look around with new eyes. I kept on

working for the same business and continued to save. When I took a trip to Madrid for a week, I became aware of a new and improved version at the helm. It wasn't quite the authentic me, but it was someone I trusted to do the right thing.

I was with an agency that placed lecturers in colleges; they contacted me for a lecturer's job whilst on holiday. I kept looking at the offer and emailed back that I would attend an interview, then turned off my phone and put it in the hotel room's safe for the duration of my holiday and tried to stop thinking about anything. On the penultimate day of my holiday, I bought *El Pais* to read and on the front cover was a picture of a crashed plane, so I took a coach home instead of my flight.

At the interview I was told that the construction section was brand new and needed setting up. I accepted the challenge.

A new instructor was hired for the department; I sensed a demon in him from day one.

One day, the demon in him complained to managers

that I was bullying him. I was suspended for two weeks with full pay as an investigation took place. I flew to Spain. When I returned, I found a letter on the floor. It explained that they could find no cause of bullying.

When I returned to work, an aggravated version was at the helm and *his* only modus operandi was to freak the accuser out, which *he* did. I was called to another meeting where they gave me another letter, and before they said anything else, I told them that I was well aware of the procedure and walked out.

Whose fault is this? Is it mine? I have always been intelligent, or reasonably so. But my intelligence was out of kilter with my soul as so many different versions took the helm. I had educated myself, but I hadn't taken complete control of myself, which is wisdom and far more important than intelligence or cleverness. I realised this and thought all my fighting and struggles had been in vain. All I had learned was no use to me because I had not learned how to combine all aspects into a cogent working unit. I had spent my life on the hoof, like a wild pony, neither taming nor disciplining its potential or exuberance. I was either playful, running wild, or skittish. Some people and opportunities tried to draw close at the shear exuberance and endearing look, but often I would unexpectedly hoof them hard before galloping over the fields and out of sight.

That version spent his time drinking, having nightmares, and raging. It was the only time any version went so low as to attempt suicide.

He decided to take a handful of strong prescription pills and left the bedsit. *He* bought vodka, then walked to a patch in the woods. It was secluded enough, although it backed onto a golf course. On a large fallen tree, *he* began the popping of pills and swigging from a bottle. Occasionally *he* made out golfers through the trees. It was a beautiful day. Sunbeams fell through leafless gaps in the trees like heavenly rain. It felt both eerie and beautiful.

It was the calmest *he'd* felt for so long and considered the decision well made. Memories ceased. The last thought of significance was that this must be what true meditation is.

When *he* woke, the sun was weaker. There was a brief discontinuity of *his* surroundings before perception returned. *He* felt an early evening breeze roll over *him* like a wave. *He* watched tall grass bowing to the wind. *He* laughed, felt better, lighter, and more energetic, silly, too. *He* was hungry. *He* stood up and walked to a local cafe and ordered double egg and chips, two slices of bread and butter, and a cup of tea.

Forking chips into a slice of bread came the realisation that this wasn't an attempt at ending *it*. After all, the drugs and drink taken were not too dissimilar to a concoction consumed on a decent night out. *He* was just feeling sorry for *himself*, no more than that.

Although there was no bed or furniture in *his* place, there were many books. I remember previous versions today by scanning *our* bookshelves. A book ushers in memories of when and where a version bought it, along with his situation and state of mind. The books stand as a diary as much as a library. Some receipts remain within the books for official confirmation of time and date.

No matter where any version went, no matter how well or ill, no matter the situation, each one was charged with taking them to the next place. The purpose was hope that the next version just might find that piece of knowledge as the key to unlock the mind and set *us* free. There were novels, philosophy, foreign language books, religion, spiritual, travel, self-development, and poetry.

I picked up a *Bible* and started to flick through it. Once again, I returned to the story where Jesus encountered the wild and crazy man who had broken free from his chains. I still wanted to be healed from the outside just like him.

I put the *Bible* down and started to picture myself as the crazy man full of demons without too much effort. The picture was photographic. I played the part. From that moment my mind began to think with increasing clarity for the first time in too long. The next thought was of a book I'd bought in a second-hand shop called *They Shall Expel Demons,* by Derek Prince. It took me a while to hunt it down because the books were strewn against the wall haphazardly. All of *us* have been attracted to strange, spiritual books.

I began to read and didn't stop until I found myself too tired to read on. What hooked me from the start was how the author explained how he had lived with depression for many years and just assumed that it was part of who he was, like I assumed mind pain was a part of me.

I started to accept that there just might be demons. I had nothing to lose and much to gain. The author wrote that not every affliction has to be a demon, and mainly you could tell if it was one if it spoke to you. When I am at my best, I feel energised, strong in thought, and light in body and step. My eyes sparkle when I look in the mirror. I have power to create. I am unconcerned about the world. I am witty and attractive to be around. Doors begin to squeak open, coincidences happen with serendipitous regularity, and the only hint of mischief that remains is contained in *our* shadow.

Recognising demons at work made it easier for me to label what I was dealing with. Giving a name and a picture of what I was up against, made it much easier to fight against, as no one wants to fight an unknown foe. A voice interrupted, "Come on, you don't really believe in this demon thing, do you? Soon you will be back to normal anyway".

I responded:

"I don't care whether I believe it or not. If it relieves me by representing mind pain or other mental issues as demons, then it's good. I don't need to know if it's true, only that it works".

I slept soundly that night and had a wonderful dream about opening a pirate's treasure chest. Fireflies rose and engulfed me in a flurry of light. I can only assume that the dream had some profound message, in a good way that is.

I Return to Versions of Myself

Gary Troia

Chapter 27

The secret to life is meaningless unless you discover it yourself.
W. Somerset Maugham

The following day I met with a counsellor my doctor had arranged, which soon led to a new direction and a new version emerging. My mind felt gentle and unadulterated. The sun shone benevolently on my face, and my step was light and easy. The river meandered.

When I told the counsellor how I'd been living, she told me that I might be an alcoholic. Alcohol and drugs have always been the go-to medicine for changing the feeling versions got from the consequences of mind pain. Prescribed drugs never had the same effect. Whenever *we* were prescribed them, they always made *us* feel worse, and they'd invariably be flushed down the toilet, which is strange for versions who liked to self-medicate. When she asked the question: "Do you drink too much"? I just shrugged. I was trying to formulate an answer that it was medicine to me when mind pain came, when she picked up a phone, dialled a number and gave it to me. By the time I'd put the phone down, it had been arranged that someone would pick me up and take me to an AA meeting the following morning.

Some versions of *myself* took prescribed drugs, illegal drugs, read books about the mind, healing, meditation, self-help, and listened to an array of labels foisted upon many of *them* after consulting with doctors, psychologists, psychiatrists, counsellors, friends, family members, and random characters encountered along the way. This was just another chapter lacking in an answer, but as always, I decided to give it a go.

I waited outside the block of flats wishing that I'd not agreed to it. Maybe if this had been a week ago in the dark hours of slinging back drink owing to a succession of desperate thoughts, then maybe I would be craving outside help. But I was on the up, and I didn't want to expose myself to a group. I had no idea who was coming for me or where I would be taken, and I'd already stopped drinking because the mind pain had departed.

I noticed a grey 4x4 coming down the road and thought, "This might be it". It indicated and slowed down. It was it. The man lent out the window and called my name. I felt content enough by his presence to get in. He was a middle-aged man, intelligent, and unassuming. There was a gentle aura about him. He asked me how I was feeling. I was feeling fine, allowing the river to take its course, but I said, "Okay".

The meeting was in the county of Kent, about five miles from my bedsit. A group was standing outside. None of them looked like an alcoholic. Many were smoking, so I lit up too.

Once inside, I got a cup of tea and a biscuit, then found a place to sit. The banners of the *Twelve Steps* stood tall and large like the billowing sails of a yacht. Once the formalities were out the way, the speaker told her story, then once she'd finished, everyone who wanted to share did so. I enjoyed the meeting and some of the sharing. It seemed honest and everyone who spoke was allowed time and space to finish. No one butted in. I thought that parliament could take a leaf out of this group's book when debating. I came out pleased that I had gone, although I knew that I wasn't an alcoholic, but also knew that this was a place to come and be, for a while, as it was beneficial to hear others with similar thoughts in their heads that urged them to self-medicate.

At home I felt energetic but did not know where to expend the energy. I even thought about going to the pub to celebrate and truly considered it. Instead, I went for a long walk and thought about writing. This had been a long-term thought that cropped up occasionally. I returned home and started to write a title: *A Bricklayer's Tales* over and over in different fonts. While I was writing, my mother called, and I foolishly told her I wanted to write a book called *A Bricklayer's Tales*. Without a moment's hesitation, she shot back with, "Oh, no, sounds like a terrible title".

After a couple of months going to AA meetings, I had an idea to call a manager at the training centre where I'd first taught brickwork. It was an urge that seemingly sprang from nowhere. So, I rang the manager who was pleased to receive my call.

He invited me over for a chat and said there was an opportunity to run a small training centre close to the Law Courts in central London. I was elated, but this was not the only serendipitous happening. At a meeting a few days later, I spoke to someone I was close to in AA and told him about the opportunity. His eyes lit up, and said, "I've got a small flat ten minutes' walk from where the training centre is, and I'm looking to rent it out". Considering I was in Kent and the job and flat were in central London, ten minutes' walk from each other, well, that was certainly something to think about.

Gary Troia

Chapter 28

You wear a mask and your face grows to fit it.
George Orwell

It was strange to comprehend. One week I was living alone in a bedsit without a job, the next week I found myself in a central London flat with a job that was in walking distance and had started to see a woman from AA. Was all this a jumbled coincidence, or an effect from a direct cause that I couldn't remember setting in motion?

Casting off from a familiar port and setting sail is always a combination of concern and joy. Concern in leaving the familiar behind, and joy at leaving the familiar behind.

Sometimes on Sundays I walked to Trafalgar Square, passing Charring Cross station that was so often an exit into central London for work, leisure, or book buying. In the evenings I went to AA meetings. I never gave myself time to sub-think my way back to disaster, never allowing the past to catch me up, circumventing my mind through action. It was a strange time, as I was neither completely authentic, but close enough, and nor was I rebellious and wanton, but close enough. My new situation had emerged, as they say, from out of the blue, and as I say, coming down the hill.

After three months, the small training centre unexpectedly closed. One week from that I got a call from the father of my friend who had let me his flat. He said that his son was in hospital, having fallen down a stairwell headfirst. I visited him; his head had swollen to a terrible size. A few days later I watched him being lowered into the ground in a cemetery in north London on a classic winter's day. The way the flat and the job had emerged together from out of the blue, now disappeared back into it.

I was fortunate I'd got closer to the woman from AA, so I moved in with her, but although she was lovely, kind and generous, I never felt that the relationship would last. I tried to remind myself of times versions were without a woman, and how they sometimes felt lonely. I forced myself to remember those times when alone and thinking that perhaps all my chances of meeting someone I truly cared for were used up, but it was always the same: whenever I was with a woman, I wanted to be alone, and when I was alone, I was searching for the right woman.

I looked at her and tried to find fault, but there was nothing. I tried to make myself love her, but I only got as far as caring for her. I even tried one of AA's staple sayings: *Fake it to make it.* But none of it helped because the energy match was absent, and to continue in the relationship would have become a type of hell as only empty relationships can be. I visualised my ship in the harbour. It was shipshape and primed. I moved out and rented a small flat.

I had time on my hands. I bought a good camera and spent time taking photos of flowers, trees, and rivers. Between photographs I kept a watch on the hill, waiting for something to arrive.

I had stopped going to AA meetings by this time. I

knew I wasn't an alcoholic, and I could no longer listen to those same voices in meetings telling the same stories. None of them seemed to heal because they kept on reliving the past in every meeting. I had to leave before I rebelled. On one walk around town, I received a call from my AA sponsor. He said he could no longer sponsor me as I wasn't going to meetings. I felt the mooring lines loosen a little more.

He was a good man and did things correctly in AA, and I was thankful that our time together had ended amicably because he had helped me through some troubling times. I had met others, too, who have remained in my thoughts. After the call I had a sense that a new version was about to take the helm.

On a walk I came across an art shop. I scanned the items of art accessories, finally resting on the adverts on the window. Most were about artists selling their art. But my eyes were drawn to one because it had the word Spain in it. It said: "Looking for someone to manage a refurbishment job in the south of Spain". My energy levels rose. I took a photo of the card and went for my first pint in over a year and a half. Now I could see my hands on the ropes, bending down on the quay, about to cast off.

I phoned the number. No answer. I left a message. Later that night I received a call. Two days on I was in an airport waiting to board yet another plane for Spain.

Gary Troia

Chapter 29

To-morrow is too late for anything, and he who sees his help and salvation in to-morrow shall continually fail and fail to-day.

James Allen

Airports are often a pregnant place where new versions gestate, hopeful of positive change and healing, and where new versions are literally born. At other times they are the disgraceful scenes of abject failure where reverting to type collapses in on itself once again. This time I sensed nothing at all. Just a small step back was a version with a girlfriend in a familiar town with acquaintances. Ahead were unknown faces, new locations, and nothing familiar. This was perhaps the strangest airport experience of them all, as I was uncertain about advancing; yet to retreat was forbidden.

In an airport chair by a window, a lack of expectation that usually accompanies setting out was nowhere to be found. All I could detect after searching was the witness behind everything. There were no more hiding places, the search was complete. Nothing stepped forward to take command. I was aimless. The drink on the table remained untouched. My mind searched for meaning to energise the journey but found none. Although something had descended the hill, I neither welcomed it, nor turned away from it. I was concerned at casting off, which did not bode well. A thought began to echo: Running away? Running again? No hint of the authentic self joining me on this journey was detected. But I couldn't and wouldn't back down.

The ideal, as always, was to never run away but to jump into nowhere and believe that authentic self will reveal itself.

In the sky I looked through the window at the land below and wondered how many versions had done the same, wondering about living down there because it was somewhere else. Where was I going to end up? Would the man be waiting for me? After all, it was just an advert in an art shop window.

I Return to Versions of Myself

Gary Troia

Chapter 30

Every way has a wherefore.

Shakespeare

The man was waiting for me. I discerned instantly that there was no rapport or connection between us, and it would not likely change for the better. I was disappointed, it was not a good omen. We drove to his house, which sat somewhere in the middle of nowhere, one of a group of ten similar houses. He owned two of them. I was shown to his second home where I was going to stay. He invited me to dinner that night. After a bottle of wine, I fell asleep and woke up half an hour late for dinner. I dressed and walked to his house, but he wouldn't answer the door. My job was over before it had begun.

It took two days before I spoke to him again. I was walking around the village, wondering if I could make the long walk over barren land and blistering Sun to town to buy supplies, when I spotted a woman with

231

long legs descending from a short skirt about to get into her car. I went and asked for a lift. She was French. She said "*Oui*". We couldn't converse in either English or French, so we used Spanish. Our rapport was simultaneously edgy and comforting, and by the time we reached town, we had agreed to meet in a bar after we'd done our shopping.

Then I spotted the man from the advert in a bar. We reconciled. We had a drink. The Frenchwoman joined us. Our liaison was over before it had begun. I stayed for a week. At the end of it I took a bus to Granada, and then another to Barcelona. I stayed overnight and visited the *Sagrada de Familia* the next morning before taking another coach to Paris and then another to London. After all that stress, I needed a holiday…

I Return to Versions of Myself

Gary Troia

Chapter 31

Hope has two beautiful daughters; their names are Anger and Courage. Anger at the way things are, and Courage to see that they do not remain as they are.

Saint Augustine

I chose Catania, Sicily. At the airport I'm calm, refreshed and looking forward to a different scene.

A taxi drops me off outside a small, neat looking hotel. My room is spacious. A large dark wooden framed bed dominates the room. A spacious window is open, and a gentle breeze persuades the net curtains to gently sway. The window looks out onto a courtyard where trees, bushes and shrubs stretch out their brown arms with intense greens hands. I switch on the radio and hear the first bars of Wagner's *Tannhäuser Overture*. Any tension I carried releases along with the passing notes of music.

On that bed the strangest feeling internalised within

me, feeling so light that I thought I was floating. When I settled into the feeling, I realised it was happiness for no other reason than itself. I hate to say it, but I feel almost embarrassed to be happy whenever it occurs, and when it comes, I sweep it immediately under a rug.

I get up and head out, taking a coffee and a *cannolo* in a café in the square close to my hotel. I felt so good and there was so much I wanted to do but didn't know which way to go, so I just walked and walked and took in the sites. From an apartment block emanates Pink Floyd's *Brian Damage*. It is loud, but the speakers are so good that it sounds fantastic. The day is turning to dusk when I decide to buy a bottle of wine to take back to the hotel. I stay in the room and have a glass whilst listening to classical music and trying to write about how I feel. I can't remember the last time I felt so happy, or if I ever have, or at least since nursery school – the pointing job was good. Many versions are just hybrids of previous incarnations, but this feeling that senses I'm about to change is distinct from them all through the lightness of my mind, yet it is far too early to indicate what this version is all about.

I feel so good that I am sleepily content and retire to bed with *The Rough Guide to Sicily,* looking out for things I would like to do and see. As the night goes on, I put together an itinerary: a visit to Mount Etna and buy a painting from a working local artist.

The following morning, I eat breakfast, then phone a company that does tours in a Land Rover to Mount Etna.

After breakfast I set out to find the artist's studio I read about and finally find it. I walk in to hear jazz playing. The artist hears me come in and is pleased when I say I want to buy something. First, he offers me a drink, and we relax. I notice that he is an abstract painter. I like his style. Time becomes irrelevant and we get talking about his time living in London and other subjects after uncorking a bottle of red wine. I finally decide on a piece, an abstract of blues and faded reds. He asks if I've been to Taormina. That is where he lives and offers me a lift.

I took the painting back to my hotel and return. We drive to Taormina and have a drink before saying goodbye. I stay for a while and look around before getting the train back to Catania.

The following morning I'm waiting outside for the ride to Mount Etna. Soon a young woman pulls up and asks if I have booked. When I get in, she says there are three more people to pick up. We pick up three Neapolitans. Fortunately, they all speak English, which takes the pressure off my child-like Italian. We drive up the volcano as far as we can, but because of inclement weather and thick cloud, the driver says she can go no higher. Instead, we stop and get out and are given hard hats before entering an old lava tunnel.

We get back in the car and start to descend the volcano, when I see a small silver-grey fox that seems to be watching me at the side of the track. I am so moved and somehow connected to it that I ask the woman to pull over. We all get out and take photos as it just sits there like a dog without fear or concern.

As we drive off, I turn my head and silently say

goodbye. It is still watching. I don't know why but it has a profound effect on me. Because we never got too far up the volcano the driver suggests that we all go for a meal in a good restaurant. The meal is delicious, and the Neapolitans buy some good wine.

That night I lay in bed and can't not stop thinking about that fox. It is strange to think that it had a message for me, but I am almost certain that it did, and if it did not, then I am moved enough to find one. I let my mind go and because it relaxes, I conclude that I can no longer blame anyone or anything for any of my situations.

On the way back to the airport I am chatting away in Italian to the driver, still feeling free and happy. In the airport a sense of deflation begins, as the holiday is over, but I catch myself and steady my ship as I must remain on course.

Gary Troia

Chapter 32

People are children.

Herman Hesse

Although I no longer went to AA, a builder that did, phoned to ask if I was looking for work. I wasn't, but decided to take him up on his offer, as the money would come in handy before starting my teaching again.

The job was to build a large garage to house the client's collection of Ferraris. The bricks were carefully chosen, and the mortar was to be a specific shade of light red, close to pink. My first day was spent building small panels of bricks with different amounts of red dye then let them dry so the ideal colour could be selected. I knew I was going to like this job, as there were going to be arches and the bed joints raked out. In other words, he wanted an exceptional job rather than a hurried job, and the money we were paid mirrored that. I bought a large bag of grass and a bike, as the journey to work from where I lived was through pleasant country lanes.

I went to work in a trance. Worked in a trance. Lived in a trance. Twenty-four hours a day in a trance. I liked being in a trance. It suited me. Every version experiences a trance-like state at some point within each of their timeline of incidences, but this was constant, enjoyable – almost refreshing to allow this way of being to see me through the days. It was close to my authentic self, and far from debilitating personality traits, demons, mind pain and suffering, leaving just the witness at the back of everything to note what took place.

I became fit. I smoked a joint before leaving for work in the morning and lit one up for the way home, stopping in a field of wheat to smoke it. I didn't smoke in the day, as I didn't want to tempt the guy who I was working with as he also went to NA (Narcotics anonymous).

I turned the repetition of laying brick after brick into a meditative practice. I was uninterested by the conversations of the other workers about football and women and made out I knew nothing about either.

Previous versions used to bother with football. *They* thought *they* had found *their* tribe as young men. The tribalism and sporadic violence that flared up used to excite *them*. I look back at that time and see how far away *they* were from being authentic. When my mother mentioned she was marrying the new man on a Saturday, a version replied that *he* wouldn't be able to manage the wedding itself because of the three o'clock kickoff but would be more than happy to make the reception. I look back at being obsessed by football as a pitiful stab at belonging to something that was outside the dreariness of everyday life. The last time I went to a football match, I got what Orwell wrote in his essay *The Sporting Spirit*:

"…films, football, beer and above all, gambling filled up the horizons of their minds. To keep them in control was not difficult".

My mind has been rewired. I've read many books on how you can rewire the brain, but the best analogy for me is to change your habits by rewiring your brain was like walking through a field of long grass. You can see the sway the first time it is walked. But if you continue walking that way, time after time, it becomes a path. In this way one changes by persistence.

The same applies to habits, addictions or anything else you want rid of, just stop walking the habitual paths and soon they will grow over and there will be no trace of that path. That is how I see fundamental change able to take place. If you keep on walking the same paths you are going to end up in the same place doing the same things with the same people.

I looked in the mirror one evening and caught my eyes staring back at me. They were clear and deep. It made me smile. My body had lost fat, whereas my bank account was doing the opposite. I could give up work for a few months and do what I wanted, but I let the indulgence of that thought wither and die and continued in the way of the trance.

It continued for months. When I returned home one evening, I flicked through my emails. I had joined an internet dating site, but apart from a couple of responses, what caught my eye was an offer of a job from a recruitment company asking if I would be interested in helping a new construction department open. I didn't know if I had snapped out of my trance, or whether my mind had somehow extended, but I felt different, nevertheless.

Many versions have expanded, some have contracted, but this version had a new sense of vigor and verve about him. I calculated my position. I had kept a bricklaying job continuously for over seven months – something that no version had ever done before. I had no arguments or fallouts with anyone; there had been no mind pain, nor much mental disruption of any description, only a trace of the mildest kind.

Now I was about to start work as a teacher again, and just like when that version flew to the U.S., everything panned out like an already authored story. I just read my lines and tried to be original.

It went so well that I moved closer to work into a flat overlooking the Thames.

Gary Troia

Chapter 33

I do not know the thing I am, and therefore do not know what I am doing, where I am, or how to look upon the world or on myself.

A Course in Miracles

I joined the local gym. Swimming lengths, aware that my improved thinking, visualising of goals, and acting towards those goals with discipline, was finally paying off. In response to that, after finishing a length and resting my arms on the side of the pool, I heard a whisper,

"Yeah, but how long before the mind pain starts again"?

I was foolish to ignore that warning and swam more lengths. And I ignored it for another two years even though the script was no more because the play had finished.

But there was still a good team, and it was easy to work with them, and easy to let things continue as they were; yet because things went well, I ignored signs of pending trouble and lost sight of discipline and insight. Old habits and coping with mind pain were being dealt with in the old ways of self-preservation.

I went from being vibrant to functional, which brought the once pleasant experience of working to hum drum days that seemed to drag much longer than they once did, wishing like the old days on site for time to mark the end of a working day.

I should have left and moved on. Most of the time I let the unstructured plot unfold however it went. Then the day arrived when I climbed to the top of my helter-skelter, sat on a mat, and slid all the way down to the bottom after violently losing both my temper and the helm as an unstable version took them over.

Yet before things got worse, I managed to leave before all was lost. I went sick. The occupational doctor signed me off indefinitely. It was one of the best decisions ever made. What came next was a combination of mind pain, a disparate crew and a demented captain. It was a terrible combination that led to a tumultuous, storm-tossed time.

Back in the flat overlooking the river was a raging maniac. And *he* was getting worse. *He* went and bought enough alcohol for a party and proceeded to have one.

The darkness that descended was like nothing before.

Alongside those dark disturbing days came an external light in the form of a woman called Marina who prevented a major disaster. We had been friends for a long time, and we were getting closer without me realising it. She was a fellow lecturer at the college who taught hairdressing. She started to visit to see if *he* was okay. She was brave because later she said *his* eyes were like pools of molten lava. I have emerged from dark phases before but without her it might not have happened that time.

I began to see a specific demon everywhere I went. It was in the supermarket, a restaurant, on the street –

everywhere! It was sometimes male, and sometimes female, and it was making me angry.

I've often read that the qualities you most despise in others are those that you despise most in yourself. I decided to forgive *it;* but it wasn't easy.

After a time, I detected the presence of this demon attached to me like a furious flame raging and rushing at the world.

For a week or more I was on fire and in utter turmoil. My nights were spent in a frightening vision of being consumed by the fire, and my days were spent wanting to destroy the demon before it destroyed me. And I continued to see *it* because I was looking for *it.*

I began to watch for *it* and became familiar with *its* behaviour. Marina would come most days, and this helped to pull me back to reality.

With her help, I managed to settle and for the first time I told her about my demons and mind pain. She understood by allowing me to rest and took care of me. It was the first time I had told anyone truly about mind pain, and it was the first time anyone had helped me recover from a bout of it.

Gary Troia

Part 3

Gary Troia

Chapter 34

For suppose you should think that a man had had a long
voyage who had been caught in a raging storm as he left the
harbour, and carried hither and thither and driven round and
round in a circle by the rage of opposing winds? He did not
have a long voyage, but a long tossing about.

Seneca

I untied the mooring lines, then sailed away from my
flat and job, out into open water. I was officially with
Marina, living with her and her child in a small,
unpleasant flat.

I went for a walk in winter rain, raindrops stinging my
cheeks and hands. I came to a pub and took shelter.
It was empty but for two men at the bar. There was
an open fire. I ordered a drink and sat close to
crackling, shifting logs. At first my thoughts were
bleak and gloomy, matching the window-framed
picture outside.

But soon my hands and face began to relax as the fire began to thaw them. A ray of light burst through onto the pub carpet. Outside clouds of gloom made way for the sun. And with the change of the external weather picture my thoughts changed too, no longer bleak but hopeful. A smile arrived, and then I thought how lucky I was to have this woman in my life. We had been long-term friends from college and now I could see how different my thoughts about her were. I called Marina and invited her for a drink.

That night I had a dream that was as powerful as the dream of the open casket emitting fireflies. I walked through a dark and empty carpark, heard crunching and cracking as I went. At first, I couldn't make it out, but soon a chink of light caught my attention. I looked down and saw that the noise was coming from me stepping on broken glass. My feet were bleeding, although I didn't feel pain. I stopped and looked closer. I saw different versions of myself reflected in each shard of glass. I also recognised emotions, mistakes, attitudes, behaviour twisted out of shape by drugs and alcohol, egotistic gurning, low self-esteem…it went on, and it wasn't just poor reflections I was perceiving, it was laughter, pride and foolishness in something or other that I had chased but soon saw as nothing but meaningless illusions.

In my mind I held a magnifying glass to the world, but instead of seeing things clearer, larger, and in more detail, everything was distorted and jumbled like I was viewing it through a kaleidoscope. After the dream, I woke and stayed awake until morning arrived and thought of nothing but the shattering sound of the smash my life had made.

Gary Troia

Chapter 35

Yea, I shall return with the tide.

Khalil Gibran

The following morning Marina took her son Jamie to school and then went to work. I stayed in the flat and could not stop thinking about the night before. Something had changed. I had only ever known myself through a succession of versions and fleeting moments of authenticity. I had created mental constructs of who I had been in my journey through this life, but they never lasted long.

Close by the ugly flat were fields and a lake. I took off and walked around it for hours. I recalled some of the shards of glass from my dream. I felt for those versions and blessed them all. At first, I felt empty, abandoned, concerned, but soon felt that I should leave all the shards wherever they were, and determined to keep it that way.

When I returned, Marina had a surprise, we were booked on a holiday to Spain, and while there, we were going to look for opportunities to move there. She had done this because she knew it was a dream of mine.

We had two weeks split in one-week halves. The first was spent in a luxury flat on the coast. The second in a smaller place in a complex. We found a magazine that listed property to rent and went and visited four. After seeing them we liked one and then had a drink with the estate agent. After talking with her she told Marina that the hairdressers were looking for someone. Marina left the bar and went to speak to the owner. When she came back, she had a job. One month later we moved to Spain.

On the day of our flight to a new life, I sat and looked at Marina. She had given up everything to follow my dream. She had never done anything remotely like it before. She'd bought into my dream. We burned our bridges, cutting ties with all we knew. I flicked back through memory banks and saw myself in airports waiting for a flight to a new land, but this was a different departure, a different journey, and a completely different course, because I was not alone.

Gary Troia

Chapter 36

It is the mind which is tranquil and free from care which can roam through all the stages of its life: the minds of the preoccupied, as if harnessed in a yoke, cannot turn around and look behind them.

Seneca

We flew to Spain with a home and a job already secured. The only major thing remaining was getting Jamie into a Spanish school. On the plane I remembered how many times I had thought about returning to Spain, and how many thoughts it had taken, sometimes dreaming, sometimes willing, wasted wishing, and now those mental seeds had taken root, and had begun to display like a new plant revealing its purpose from the soil.

I could not see it then but moving to Spain was an end to the past and the beginning of my return to the present. It was a breakaway for both Marina and me. I love breakaways, but Marina had never done anything of the sort before and rightly carried some hesitancy and trepidation with her. Marina told me that if we hadn't got away when we did, she might have had a breakdown, as all her supposed friends and colleagues had an opinion about us, and they all advised her that I would be a disaster for her and her child, and so they stopped at nothing in their words to defame me.

One called me a psychopath, another thought I might have AIDS, owing to the *number* of women I'd slept with...

Instead of enjoying our new start, I was gnashing my teeth in the day, and grinding them at night with thoughts and dreams of crushing the ones who had made Marina so unhappy, until one day I started to reread *A Course in Miracles,* and in Lesson 8, I came across this sentence, "The one wholly true thought one can hold about the past is that it is not here". And from that moment not only did those people begin to diminish then vanish, but it was also the catalyst for the rest of the incidents in my life to fade away. Yet a clear-out of old thoughts and behaviour would not come easy or immediately, but at least I was aware of my purpose and determined to achieve it.

It wasn't an easy task, but with each hurdle and obstacle we managed to find a way through. It also helped that although I had a small stipend from England, it wasn't enough to just leave and runaway for either of us, so we had no choice but to battle through our problems – mainly my problems of mind pain, twisted ideas, and disregard for social conventions. Spain was the forge where I began to temper my impurities and irregularities into something resembling a decent man before turning to my goal of authenticity.

The better I thought, the more my environment and aspects of my life changed. I started to write for an advertising company, and then I got a job writing for a football magazine. And one-day Marina met a man (whilst cutting his hair) that owned a magazine. I went to meet him and got a job writing a monthly article about life in Spain. He said it had to be around one thousand words long, which I took to heart, making the articles exactly one thousand words long. This work helped with my editing and having to meet deadlines, which was good practice and training. When I got my hands on that first issue, the joy I felt when I saw my article, remains one of my most memorable moments of my life.

I Return to Versions of Myself

Gary Troia

Chapter 37

Every outward trial is the replica of an inward imperfection.
James Allen

It had been a great adventure, but all adventures must end. Together we had accomplished a long-held goal of mine. Now it was time to return the favour. Marina's goals were not as singularly selfish as mine. She wanted a proper home (we had no real security in Spain), Jamie to complete his exams in England, and a baby; and although all were agreed by me in principle, I never truly believed that a baby would emerge.

I suppose the thought of having a child was not only an alien concept to me but had become that way because of the problems I carried with me. Even at that point, with all the work I had done on myself, I just felt that I was too irresponsible for such a responsible task of bringing up a well-formed child.

We returned like refugees to our country with no money, not even enough to buy a drink on the plane home. We survived on very little. I spent my days walking a large circuit around where we lived, after managing to rent a bungalow. Sometimes I got so frustrated that I just kept walking until I tired myself out, chafed my thighs, and couldn't take another step. Once, I walked for so long that Marina was about to ring local hospitals to find out if I'd had an accident.

Marina owned a house which had to be sold, so we knew there was something about to come down the hill. I had difficult times in that bungalow with mind pain and frustration, but I started to deal with them by looking at myself, watching my behaviour, and changing negative thoughts to positive. I knew that I wanted to remain with Marina, yet still I had to deal with my habitual thoughts about getting away and being alone. I soon regarded these thoughts as remnants from a previous version, so I was no longer guilty or worried about them, I just accepted the dark side and let the thoughts fly away. I was learning to dig in and hold the line in the face of enemies I once feared, the main one then being the looming shadow of taking on the massive responsibility of a family.

I remembered those two bricklayers having a family life and often doubting that I ever could, but sometimes, in times of strength and high vibration, the vision was not only achievable, but necessary. That thought was occasional, but the seed of that thought had taken hold and was beginning to show signs of fruition in a seldom used part of my mind. I wasn't advanced societally in any real sense, but I was coping better than I'd ever done. Also, having someone who understood mind pain and being able to talk to her about it was something that I could no longer live without. It was essential. As we went on, I started to exchange loneliness and isolation for closer relationships, and anger and frustration for peace and tranquillity. But let me be clear: these were fragile and delicate seedlings then, and a sudden change in the weather might well have destroyed the crop in one fatal outburst.

Gary Troia

Chapter 38

Aemelia

A happy family is but an earlier heaven.
George Bernard Shaw

The day arrived when Marina's house was sold. We had a big decision to make. Were we going to build our lives in our hometown of London, or somewhere else?

My mother lived in Dorset, and when we visited, we used to stop in Winchester for a break and something to eat. One time, sitting and eating our lunch on the grass in front of Winchester Cathedral, I said, "You know what, I love it here, we should make this our home. Let's make it happen".

One evening Marina showed me a house for rent in Winchester. It was pink and detached. We went and viewed it and discussed at lunch what we were going to do. The decision was unanimous, so, within a month, we had moved to Winchester. It was a couple of weeks before Christmas, and Winchester is a magical place at that time of the year, as there is a Christmas market and an ice-skating rink. I have never been happier about a move. Just before the holidays began, I went to the market to buy Marina a handbag for Christmas. The woman at the stall mentioned that I was the most joyful person she'd seen all day. I walked away thinking that no one had ever called me joyful before. I bought a cup of mulled wine, sat on a bench and indulged myself briefly of the past I'd lived before bringing myself back to the present, taking in now again. The contrast was stark. I shivered momentarily at the thought that if I'd been a person who was unaware or lacking in persistence about needing to change and acting on that realisation, I might not have kept going long enough to reach this moment.

We married at Winchester Registry Office. Marina had no persuading to do for us to get married, but she did have when it came to our honeymoon. She wanted to book a cruise with Cunard around the

Mediterranean. I thought it was going to be boring and dull, full of pensioners in ill-fitting gowns and suits. But when we arrived in the cab at Southampton docks, I saw the ship which had the instant effect of elevating my entire thought process about Marina's choice and thinking that this was going to be a lot better than I had envisioned. As soon as I got in the terminal, I decided to write an account about it, and so I wrote and published my first cruise book, *Through the Porthole*.

This has been a constant theme with Marina – getting me out of my comfort zone, and most of the time, me loving the new zone. Often, she has entered my office and announced she has booked something or other, and I like that.

The day Marina announced to me she was pregnant, startled me, as the thought of having a real child was almost too much for me to comprehend, as I had just about become comfortable with the idea; but it also coincided with some shutters that were slammed down at early stages of my story being raised in celebration of new life. I didn't know it then, but a rigorous spring-clean was about to take place within me in places that had long been ignored and disregarded.

As Marina's belly expanded, my mind began to perceive that a baby was truly no longer just an abstract talking point – she was on her way! This was going to impact my life like nothing before. I used to assume I'd live alone for the span of my part in this world, as relationships of any kind seemed impossible to me, and I had accepted that realisation with good grace. Yet I had met Marina and we have been together already longer than I imagined, and longer also of any previous relationships with all other women combined. She had accepted my mind pain and helped me through turbulent times. Alongside that, I had made major breakthroughs, many of which would not have been overcome without her help. So having once decided to give up on relationships altogether, another one was about to join us on our journey.

I Return to Versions of Myself

Gary Troia

Chapter 39

There can be no doubt that you will reach your final goal.

A Course in Miracles

I used to lay in bed with Marina at night, amazed and concerned that there were two in one lying next to me.

Sometimes I would put an ear to her belly and listen to what was going on inside. It used to disturb and unnerve me that our child was living and growing inside. Something so small yet huge in consequence was heading my way, and nothing would ever be the same again. On the plus side, I kept telling myself, at least I am taking this quite seriously.

On the 23rd of November, our little girl was born, but it wasn't an easy entry into the world for any of us. The day started well. Marina, the midwife, and me in a room at the Maternity Ward in Winchester Hospital. Classical music was playing, the three of us doing a general knowledge quiz from a book.

Marina asked me to get her a coffee from a shop in the main hospital. The mellow scene I'd just left was a completely different play when I returned. Three people had turned into six. Marina was in bed shivering and shaking uncontrollably like she had hypothermia. They debated then concluded that a caesarean section was the way to go. After that everything went into rapid motion. Marina was wheeled to the theatre, and I was given a gown and hat.

I was holding Marina's hand and before long I caught what looked like a skinned rabbit being held up. I was expecting our baby to be handed to her mother, but another medical professional came in with a cart and placed her on it and wheeled her away.

Things got worse. Marina was also taken away.

Now I was separated from them both. I didn't know where they took our baby but was told after an uncomfortable wait that she was in the Special Care Baby Unit. From that moment on, I began to pray that they would both get better, and I was prepared to give anything so that our baby recovered. It was a new selfless feeling that I'd never experienced before. Eventually I was allowed to see Aemelia in the unit. There were tiny tots in there and at last I saw Aemelia in an incubator with so many wires and other bits attached to her, my heart sank, but my will for her to get better became my sword of strength to remain strong. The doctor later told me Marina had sepsis, which she passed to Aemelia and they would both need much care.

On the way home I walked through Winchester late at night with the Christmas lights mocking my pain. I went home alone and thought how different this should have been. On the night of our daughter's birth, I stayed awake through the night in utter turmoil of what my wife and daughter were going through, but I girded myself, steered away from negativity by ardent prayer and supplication to any deity that just might be listening.

Gary Troia

Chapter 40

It is easier to build strong children than to repair broken men.
Frederick Douglass

For the next week and a half, I went to the hospital in the morning, and returned home in the evening. I visited Marina first, then down to the Special Care Baby Unit to see Aemelia, then back with Marina for most of the day. Before I left, I would go and say goodbye to Aemelia. After three or four days I was allowed to hold my daughter in my arms, and I could not stop (nor did I want to) tears from rolling down my cheeks. I talked to her about her new bedroom that we had decorated, and of all the things we were going to do as a family. I told her that she must get well so we can all go home together. I described her lovely mum (they had still not met each other formerly) and how grateful we were to be her parents.

As the days went by, both mother and daughter got better together and the many wires that were once attached to Aemelia started to diminish until there were none, and when I next visited the hospital, the little one was in a cot beside her mother. Aemelia recovered to be a healthy baby with no problems whatsoever, and I believe in prayer and the incredible dedication of the nurses and doctors in the Special Care Baby Unit at Winchester Hospital.

I Return to Versions of Myself

Gary Troia

Chapter 41

The most interesting information comes from children, for they tell you all they know and then stop.

Mark Twain

It would be crass to mention what I have achieved, but I will concede that I have accomplished dreams I once thought were nothing but dreams and accomplished goals that used to seem like fanciful wishes.

I still get feelings of unease and bouts of problematic mind pain, but these feelings are more to do with wanting to be a better man, a better father, a better husband, and are nothing more than frustration that my vision of myself isn't materialising quick enough. These are warnings to me that I am not living up to the values and goals I have set myself. I still make plenty of mistakes, but I see them as that: just errors, and so they do not carry the seeds of guilt that must be dealt with later.

There was a dark period of mind pain where I got arrested and spent the night in jail, and just about resisted a descent down my highest ever helter-skelter; yet even that terrible time has ultimately strengthened me.

The reason I wrote this account is to finally deposit my burdensome weight of guilt, poor programming, trauma, bad choices, negative thinking, and maudlin memories, a cargo that almost destroyed my ship. I nearly capsised, almost sank.

But these final words are where I get to unload it all. The cargo is the past. I have been sailing with it for too long, and every port where I thought I might unload it, turned into a mirage, a false dawn.

But now a port has been reached. The cargo unloaded by giving an account of it. I have missed out many turbulent times and a few happy moments, but this is not an autobiography. I now feel that writing an account every few years might be the way to go, as no therapist, psychologist, or psychiatrist is ever going to untie, and release twisted and knotted memories as only you can when looking inside and making sense of them on paper.

I've never experienced continuous joy until lately. I no longer want to wear a mask, nor a particular attire to match it. I only want to be the authentic Self. The shutters I slammed down so long ago have been raised to allow rejuvenating air to sweep through and accept light and warmth. And although I am now open, it is still essential to block disruptive thoughts and influences entering my home by being vigilant and not opening the door to them. Yet I am not the finished article.

So how will I recognise this unwavering authentic Self? Logion 84 in *The Gospel of Thomas* says this about it:

"When you see

Your true likeness,

You rejoice".

Until then, I'm confident enough to say...

There were many things wrong with me, but fewer than before. My behaviour was often inappropriate, but it's better than before. My mind has caused me pain, but less so than before.

The End of a past...

I Return to Versions of Myself

Gary Troia

ABOUT THE AUTHOR

Gary Troia was born in southeast London and studied Spanish and Philosophy at Middlesex University and the Universidad de Deusto.

In 2010, he left behind a career in education and moved to a small Spanish village, where he began his lifelong dream of writing.

His first book, Spanish Yarns and Beyond, is a humorous account of his time in Spain. 'A great play on words, witty and well written,' was how one reviewer described the book.

A Bricklayer's Tales, published in 2013, is a collection of ten tales, including: Angel Dust, the peculiar story of a man whose new life in America leads to conversations with Ancient Greek philosophers. Mrs. McClintock, an absurd farce in which a Glaswegian couple retire to Spain, and A Bricklayer's Tale, the story of a disillusioned, alcoholic bricklayer.

Since then Gary has gone on to write eleven books.

Gary now lives in Hampshire, with his partner Marina and his daughter Aemelia where he continues to write.

Gary Troia